-- INTRODUCTION --

This is a funny book. You don't need any college to enjoy it. The humor appeals to anyone who likes to laugh: homemakers, bank presidents, bricklayers, beauticians, people from every walk of life. Honest!

Most of these true episodes (77% happened to me personally) took place at Northwestern University after World War II, and many make reference to Phi Delta Theta Fraternity. I still boost my school and my fraternity -- belong to the Alumni Association and the N-Club. But, you don't have to know details about either of those wonderful institutions to enjoy this book.

During my time at Northwestern we studied hard, however, opportunities for fun and sport were limited only by our imaginations. You'll probably identify with me and read about yourself as we experience the universal happenings of life, on the humorous side.

Enjoy the book anytime. Take it to bed with you and read a couple of episodes. You're sure to fall asleep with a smile on your face even if you're sleeping alone.

--- Lee Riordan

COLLEGE BRED
Or A Four
Year Loaf

LEE RIORDAN

R Riters Publishing
P.O. Box 93111
Milwaukee, Wisconsin 53203

Library of Congress Catalog Number
87-060675

International Standard Book Number
0-9618266-0-6

First Original Edition

Published in the United States
of America

by

R Riters Publishing
P.O. Box 93111
Milwaukee, Wisconsin 53203

ACKNOWLEDGMENT

The author wishes to thank the following people without whom this book would have been impossible.

Emily, Helen, Roberta, Jay, Barbara, Jean, Mary, Lori, Skip, Paul, Tubby, Stan, Fatso, Stoutso, Bob, Frank, Lee, Steve, Richie, Joe, Ed, Alex, Rudy, Dorothy, Sue, Maureen, Art, Don, Rick, Joan, Beth, Tom, Glen and many others.

Additional copies are available at
selected book stores and by

-- MAIL --

$8.95 each (includes postage and
handling) <u>from</u> the author (check or
money order, please)

Lee Riordan
P.O. Box 93111
Milwaukee, WI 53203

```
 _____
|                                |
| Name.........................  |
|                                |
| Address......................  |
|                                |
| City.........................  |
|                                |
| State.............Zip........  |
|                                |
| # of copies..................  |
|                                |
| Amount enclosed $............  |
|_____|
```

EPISODES

.... Cont'd >>

Sorry, that's all for now.....

A thirty inch waist topped by a forty-six inch chest, all this packed into a nice fitting tennis outfit. Yes, I figured I appeared pretty imposing next to the Northwestern University tennis courts. My second place "Mr. Milwaukee" legs, were on display like the rest of me. Admiring glances from the women in the area rolled over me in ever increasing waves.

I'd only been on the campus for about a week, but the courts were supposed to be some of the best in the country, and I had wanted to look them over - and, perhaps find some coeds who were interested in tennis or other activities. I bounced two balls simultaneously with my racket, a trick I'd picked up while winning a high-school letter.

"Well how yo'all good lookin!" I spun around to gape at one of the prettiest blonds I'd ever seen. My bouncing balls were quickly forgotten in her lovely smile. "Ah

haven't seen you around here
before"

"Well, you --- you see," I
stammered trying not to let my eyes
wander over her. "I, er, I only
started here this quarter."

Her smile widened. "That
explains it then. Ah sure would
have noticed you before." By now I
was noticing her all over. She
extended her hand. "Mah name's
Bobby Jane."

"Well, mine's Lee," I said,
taking her hand. It felt
diminutive, yet strong.

"Lee," she echoed. "Why, that's
an unusual name for a Yankee, but I
love it. You'd probably guess he
was my favorite general."

"Well, you see my Father's a
Civil War buff, and he's always
admired General Lee."

"Your Daddy must be a very smart
man," she said. "Would you like to
play a little?" Her eyes bored into
mine in a way that promised a very
interesting future.

"Why sure," I replied and I
watched her as she danced onto the
court.

Her tennis outfit was pure silk.
I knew, because I'd sold women's

clothes. The sun had kissed her skin to a rosy bronze color and bleached her hair almost platinum. She wore it tied back in a single braid that provocatively caressed her seat.

<u>Wow</u>, I thought, <u>I'll</u> <u>take</u> <u>it</u> <u>easy</u> <u>on</u> <u>her</u>. <u>This</u> <u>could</u> <u>lead</u> <u>to</u> <u>something</u> <u>big</u>.

"Would you like to volley a while?" I called to her.

"No, General Lee, how about we play a couple of sets?"

"O.K." I said, somewhat surprised. "Whatever you say."

She held up a ball, "Would you like to volley for serve, Love Bug?"

"Why no," I replied, "why don't you start in?" After all, I was a gentleman and I didn't want to make her look too bad.

Without another word she tossed the ball above her head. A split second later it screamed into my court, exploding away from my backhand.

She scored four straight aces. "Ah guess it's just beginner's luck," she yelled as I finally got my chance to serve. Sure, I felt upset, but my serve had the reputation of being a real cannonball. I put all my 200 pounds into the first one.

Her return hit my left toe. I hadn't seen it, but I sure felt it. "Are you alright, Love Bug?" she called.

"Oh yeah," I said through gritted teeth, "just fine."

She beat me 0-6,0-6. She produced a thick towel from an athletic bag I hadn't noticed before. It said "Bobby Jane" on it in big letters. She handed me the towel. "Here, you're really sweating. I don't want you to catch a cold, Love Bug."

I wiped my face and arms. She didn't seem to be perspiring at all. I returned the towel and said with a slight tone of bitterness, "Thanks for the lessons."

She beamed with sheer feminine pride, "Ah swear we all have our off days. Anytime you want to play again, I'm at the Gamma Phi House."

Somehow I didn't care where she lived. "Well, I have to go out to football practice," I said, picking up my equipment.

"Football!" she said, "why that's really thrilling. I'll be

cheering for you, Lee. I bet you're really good at <u>that</u>!"

When I returned to my Fraternity House some guys were on the porch. "Hey, Lee, how was the tennis?"

"Well," I replied glumly, "you guys won't believe this, but some little blond doll wiped me."

They all laughed. "You must have run into the 'barracuda.'"

"The barracuda?" I asked.

"Sure, Bobby Jane. She hangs around the courts waiting for dumb unsuspecting prey like you."

They all laughed lustily. "She's the Mid-west Junior Women's Champ."

"Gee," I said, "I sure was taken. How come she's the Mid-west Champ being from the South?"

They almost fell out of their chairs laughing. "She's from the South Side of Chicago. And don't you forget it Love Bug!"

The assistant-athletic-director jammed the cigar back in his mouth and reached over to pat me on the back of my neck. "You're all set boy." he announced gruffly, "You don't have a thing to be concerned about."

I hoped he was right. We'd just been negotiating on how football was going to keep me in school after my G.I. Bill ran out. It looked O.K., but there was nothing in writing, and classes hadn't even begun.

He looked at his watch, and then at me. "You just get down to the Admissions Office, don't be late for practice, and don't worry about a thing."

My watch read 2 o'clock and practice began at 3:30 sharp. I'd already been late once this week. I assumed the lines at the Office of Admissions would be long.

Wow, had I been right! My line was about two blocks in length, stretching down Orrington Avenue. What should I do? Probably give up.

I was about to do just that when I heard my name being called by someone way up ahead. "Mr. Riordan! Where are you Mr. Riordan?"

I charged forward and found a diminutive fellow calling my name. He was wearing the same type of white tee-shirt I was with NORTHWESTERN UNIVERSITY FOOTBALL stenciled in black. "Mr. Riordan!" He called again.

"Here I am," I yelled, quickly confronting him. "I'm Riordan."

He smiled warmly, "Good, Mr. Riordan. You're next."

I couldn't believe it. My benefactor and I passed what appeared to be hundreds of students on our way to place me at the head of the line. The students seemed to view this event good naturedly. I heard the words "jock" and "football-player" mentioned a number of times. One girl even dreamily said, "Don't forget to call me after practice."

Finally I arrived at the head of the line to confront a pleasant looking lady behind a teller's window. She smiled, immediately noting my tee-shirt. "You're Mr. Riordan."

"Yes, ma'am. That's right."

"Well everything seems to be in order. You don't have a thing to be concerned about."

"Thank you ma'am," I said, recalling those same words spoken only a few minutes before.

"You're all set."

"Thank you ma'am," I repeated sincerely, and turned to go.

"Oh, Mr. Riordan," she called.

"Yes, ma'am?"

She beamed a really beautiful smile. "Please don't be late for practice."

"She's probably the most beautiful girl at Northwestern," said the first Brother.

"And, you know this school is noted for beautiful women," said the second Fraternity Brother.

"I've heard she takes two hours just to put on her makeup," said a third.

"She's been on the covers of seven magazines -- really something," said the fourth.

These four had just "fixed me up" with my first date at Northwestern and were trying to reassure me that she was a definite winner. I really wasn't worried, but they seemed determined I realize they had come up with a young lady who was above the usual.

They had! When I called for her at the sorority house, even though I was a war veteran, my knees nearly buckled. To say she was "gorgeous" would have been almost and "insulting" understatement.

Her blonde curls kissed parts of utter perfection and framed eyes of the deepest ultramarine. If any of

17

this vision were the result of two hours of preparation, I felt every second had been worth it. She appeared flawless, a masterwork of classic beauty and harmony.

Apparently, some of the other girls liked to observe her effect on a new date. They watched surreptitiously from various parts of their living room. I didn't disappoint them. I stammered my name, uttered some foolish comment about the weather, and almost fell over a coffee table while helping her insert her right arm into the left sleeve of her coat.

Going down the steps, to the car where the others waited, I adored her. As we drove along the Outer Drive to Chicago, I loved her. By the time we arrived at a posh night club, I worshipped her.

Eventually, a waiter approached our group, and I asked my "goddess" what she wanted to drink. She bathed me in the mellow sunshine of her smile and replied, "I'd like a magnum of champagne."

I turned to our waiter and shrugging said, "That'll be two beers, please - domestic."

"WAKE UP!"

"Wake Up Boy" sounds like a verbal command, but in reality it was the title of the most traumatic and dangerous job in my Fraternity. I had the title during my first year, when I was a "pledge." A "pledge" is a guy who's on probation before being initiated and becoming a full-fledged member of the Fraternity. Nobody wanted the job of "Wake Up Boy." It was an awesome responsibility.

Basically, you were responsible for the beginning of each member's day. Every evening you had to post a "Wake-Up, Sign-Up" sheet divided into times the House occupants could select: 7:00 a.m., 7:15, 7:30, and lastly 8:00 a.m. The dining room stopped serving breakfast at 7:35 and most people had a class at 8:30. As Wake Up Boy you were supposed to "wake up" some 70 guys during that one hour period, know "what's for breakfast," (a lot of guys skipped oatmeal); eat your own breakfast; and take care of the problem cases.

(Oh Lord, the problem cases!).

We all slept in "sack rooms" of varying size. Small ones sleeping eight were at each end of the second and third floors. Two much larger ones occupied the fourth floor, a huge dorm and one with twelve double deck bunks for the so-called "Psycho-Vets," fellows who were still fighting World War II. I resided there.

So, for each designated time slot on the wake-up sheet your duty took you to six separate locations. You almost had to run from room to room. Until I served in the job, I never realized people had so many ways of, and moods in -- waking up.

One day I made a diary so I'd always recall what I went through. I wanted it to be condensed but typical so I deleted the roughest curses. Most of the fellows were quite nice about being gently awakened:

7:00 a.m.

<u>Sam</u> "Sam, it's seven o'clock. You awake, Sam? It's seven."

"O.K., thanks Lee. I'm awake."

<u>Frank</u> "Frank, it's seven." He swings at me, a roundhouse right.

"Get out of here you son of a bitch!"

"Frank, you're down for seven."

"Get out of here!" he swings at me again, then starts to snore.

Larry "Larry, it's seven o'clock."
He sits straight up and clutches my arm. "Roberta, I love you. I never meant to let you down."

"Larry, you're at Northwestern. I'm waking you up at 7:00. You've got class.

"Roberta, Roberta? Oh yeh, thanks. I'm awake. I'm O.K."

Ronny "Ronny, it's seven o'clock. Seven o'clock, Ronny." He doesn't move but his eyes are open. He springs on me and forces me to the floor.

"You Kraut bastard I'll kill you." He chokes me. I fight back banging his chin.

"Ron, this is the Phi Delt House." I spit this out between chokes. "You're in school Ron."

"Yeh, O.K. I'm sorry. I'm O.K. You O.K.? Gee thanks, I'm really sorry. It won't happen again, I promise."

7:15

Ted   "Ted, it's seven-fifteen."

"What? What's wrong?"

"Ted, it's seven-fifteen. You've got to get up."

"Get outta here you jerk."

"But, it's seven-fifteen. You've got to get up."

"Well, blow it out your ass. I'm going back to sleep."

Frank   "Frank, it's seven-fifteen and you wanted up at seven."

He swings at me again, another roundhouse right. "Get out of here you son of a bitch."

"Frank you were supposed to be up at seven. It's seven-fifteen, right now."

"Get out of here!" he swings at me again, then starts to snore.

7:30

Dan   "Hey Dan, it's seven-thirty. Breakfast ends in five minutes."

"Yeh, yeh, well what's up for breakfast this morning?"

"Creamed rat-shit."

"Oh good, good, I'd never get up for oatmeal." He reaches for his robe.

22

<u>Frank</u>   "Frank, it's seven-thirty. I
tried to call you at seven, and
seven-fifteen." He simply   keeps
snoring.

I take a tube of shaving cream
out of my pocket and squeeze a
generous amount into his gaping
mouth. He blows a mess of large
bubbles that drool down the side of
his face. Then I rush down to the
dining   room   for   a   delicious
breakfast of waffles and sausage.
Everyone eating breakfast is there
because of me.

Someone has taken my board-job
so I can be Wake Up Boy. I'd rather
wash dishes anytime. At 7:50, I
fill   a bucket of   water,   and
annoint each guy listed before
8:00 a.m. and still in the sack
with a few well place drops. "You
bastard,   Riordan,"   is   an oft-
repeated phrase. I'm glad to see
Frank is up. Apparently a mouthful
of shaving cream was all it took.

8:00

<u>Chevy</u>   "Chevy, <u>it's</u> eight o'clock."
<u>He's</u> a former Flying Fortress
pilot. I've had trouble with him
before, on wake-up.

23

"Thanks Lee." He sits up, "It's sure a beautiful morning to be alive."

"Yeh, Chev, it sure is."

He smiles and says pleasantly in his mid-South accent, "Ya take care now, you hear?"

Okie   "Hey, Okie, it's eight o'clock."

"O.K., thanks, I'm awake."

"Dreaming of sex, no doubt."

"No you cretin, I said I'm awake. I'm not dreaming about sex, I'm thinking about sex." He pulls his legs out and sits there on the side of the bunk in his pajamas. "What was for breakfast, today?"

"Rat-shit, one of your favorites."

"You're right, I shouldn't have missed it."

Now, I just had time to shave and race to my 8:30 class.

"John S." was, I'm sure, the most serious problem case in the long and proud history of our Fraternity Wake Up Boys. If it weren't for them and a multitude of caring Fraternity Brothers, he never would have graduated with

24

"Distinction." In fact, he never would have come close to graduating at all.

I faced John S. when I was a Wake Up Boy. The night before he'd have a test he'd put up signs all over the House saying:

"Please be sure John S. is up by 8:00 a.m. He has a test at 8:30. Don't take no for an answer, HE MUST BE UP."

At least a dozen of these signs were erected in strategic places, especially the toilets. He talked to me the night before. "I'm pretty hard to awaken, Lee."

"I've heard you're legendary."

"Well, I'll fight, and all that," he admitted, "but once I'm awake, I'm O.K. Honest!"

"John, I've heard waking you is almost impossible."

"No, no," he protested, "I'm difficult but not impossible. Lee, you strike me as a very intelligent guy. You'll be able to handle me, I'm sure."

"I'll sure as heck try."

"Good, good! Remember, I've got to make that test."

The next morning I tried him at 7:00. He didn't move a muscle. "You'll never get him up alone," observed one of the more experienced Brothers. "You're going to need help."

At 7:15 I tried to waken him more energetically. I shouted at him. No response. I pulled his covers off. He pulled them back. A steady stream of talk had absolutely no effect.

At 7:30 I tore his bedclothes off, blankets, sheets, pillows and threw them on the floor. He actually grabbed the blankets back and returned to bed. All through this disturbance he seemed to be fast asleep and simply reacting from instinct.

During breakfast I recruited about a dozen Brothers and Pledges to help. One, who knew John S.'s problem well, said, "This guy is honestly beyond belief. He'll do anything not to wake up."

About 7:50 a bunch of us entered John S.'s sack room. "Come on John, you've got that test at eight-thirty." No response. We dumped him on the floor. He battled to get back in bed, and succeeded. I gave him my bucket of water full in his face. He shrugged it off and continued sleeping in his soaked bed.

We pulled him to the floor again and seven of us sat on him. He struggled with superhuman strength. The seven couldn't hold him down so two more jumped on. I waved one of his notices in his face. "It says here, to be sure you're up John. You've got an important test at 8:30."

Wild eyed he responded, "It's a lie. I like to write that. I was only kidding."

"Don't believe him," shouted one of the Brothers. "He always says that!"

About a dozen of us carried him, battling all the way, to the shower stalls. "You're going to make that 8:30 test John!"

"No, no," he protested vehemently.

"Make sure it's good and cold," I shouted.

One of our group tested the water. "It's freezing."

"Great!" We threw him bodily into the shower. Then we went our separate ways, preparing for 8:30 classes.

I shaved and brushed my teeth on a lower floor. Then I thought I'd check on John S. The shower on his floor was in use. <u>Had</u> <u>it</u> <u>been</u> <u>left</u> <u>on</u>?

I approached to turn it off if nobody was using it. I looked inside.

There, laying in the corner of the stall being pelted constantly by powerful sprays of frigid water was John S. -- still very much fast asleep.

"Hairbreadth Harry," it said on the back of the long plastic raincoat worn by a guy who, strangely enough, liked to call himself Hairbreadth Harry. I knew his real name <u>was</u> Harry, and he lived in a dorm just to the south.

Now, there were nearly as many money-making schemes around as guys who needed it. After all, Northwestern was a very expensive place, and not everyone had the G.I. Bill or an Athletic Scholarship. There were sandwich peddlers, hot-dog cookers, haircutters, you name it.

But, Harry had the most unusual idea for making money I'd ever seen. Every Saturday morning he'd appear at Long Field, near the very north end of the campus, with his raincoat, a shot-gun, and a big box of bird-shot shells. For a dollar, you could take a shot at Harry.

He'd stand out about fifty yards, turn around, and pull the raincoat up over his head, then his assistant would hand you the gun. Blam! "Next" -- or you could have

29

as many shots as you wanted at a buck a blast.

Some Saturdays there'd be two to three hundred guys lined up. This evidence of depravity in supposedly super intelligent university students sickened me. Sure, many of us were veterans, used to violence, however we weren't animals.

I shot at Harry only once, but I think most of my pellets missed him. I wasn't sure, but he didn't stagger at all.

Sometimes he did. He told me even with the raincoat that reached to just below his knees, the pellets really stung. For some reason, he wore only sneakers, and after being a target the lower part of his legs, especially around his ankles, would be streaked with blood. He didn't seem to mind though. His assistant managed the act carefully, never allowing an early shot, and Harry was making big money.

Eventually the crowds got so large, the University found out and the Evanston Police put an end to Harry's enterprise.

Oh, later there were a few occasions when word got around that

Harry would appear at some field in the country the next Saturday, but forced off campus, his business soon failed.

Ultimately, he graduated from Northwestern "with distinction," cum laude at most other schools.

Many of us, even his best customers, had a soft spot in our hearts for him. When a bunch of "Wildcats" sat around having a few beers, someone invariably would make a toast, "Here's to Harry, a guy who really could take a shot."

My fraternity brothers came from a wide range of family backgrounds. Norris Fester's dad was a regular army general. His family drove three different cars. General Fester had a black Lincoln convertible to run around in. However, his military duties took him to many place, so he was seldom able to use it.

Norris and I put all the cars to good use, but we especially liked the huge black job that had mountings in the front fenders for the general's four-star wired-flags.

Now, while I always had a lively interest in aviation, Fester could be classified as an airplane "nut." Anything that flew absolutely turned him on.

One day he ran up to me and excitedly announced, "There's a P-80 'Shooting Star' out at Glenview. ("Glenview" was the Illinois Naval Air Station, and the Shooting-Star was our country's first operational jet fighter.)

"Let's go out there and look it over."

"Great," I replied, "is it on exhibit or something?"

"Not a chance," said Norris shaking his head, "when they aren't flying it, it's under tight security. They've even got sentries in front of the hanger." He was in the R.O.T.C. so I tended to believe him.

"Well, I guess that rules out our seeing it."

"Oh, not at all," he assured me. "I've got a plan."

Did I know Norris Fester to be fearless? Positively! But, he was crazy too. Absolutely!

That night after he told me his "plan," I could only keep repeating, "Norris, you're crazy! You're crazy!" Since his father possessed a tank-like build, similar to mine, he had decided I should wear one of the general's uniforms, gold braided cap and all, and he'd don a navy enlisted man's whites. We'd erect the four-star flags on the Lincoln's fenders and as navy personnel of every rank snapped to surprised attention, we'd simply drive through the gates and on to the hanger for a leisurely look at the Shooting-Star.

"It'll be a piece of cake," he said confidently.

"We'll end up in Leavenworth," I shouted. "Your dad'll make sure we get at least twenty years."

"More like fifty," mused Fester, "Yeh, at least fifty, but he'll never find out."

"Maybe they'll shoot us."

"Naw, they'll be too surprised."

"Norris, I'd be even crazier than you to go in there dressed as an Army General."

"Forget it Norris."

"Listen Lee, did you ever hear of the German commando, Otto Skorzeny?"

"Well, yeh, sure I did."

"He took over control of Hungary, under the noses of about 5,000 troops, by driving into their headquarters standing exposed in a tank turret, saluting. The Hungarians were so surprised they didn't know what to do. In the confusion, with a handful of men, he took over the entire place."

"Listen, this isn't Hungary, we don't have a tank, or anybody supporting us. It'd be just you and me, with our butts hanging out ready to draw a federal rap."

"People are the same everywhere, we'll take 'em by surprise. Anyway, you could plead you're a psycho veteran," he laughed. "It'll work. Besides, I've just got to get close to that P-80."

"I don't give a damn if I never see that crate."

"Come on, where's your spirit of adventure?"

"This wouldn't be adventure, it'd be suicide."

"Hey, don't worry, it'll be fun, and we'll pull it off. You'll see."

"Count me out."

Norris unfolded a map. "Here, I've got our route traced out in green."

"Not a chance."

"Here's where we'll take off our uniforms after getting away. It's a schoolyard, where the girls will be waiting for us. Once we're behind the building I'll stop the car, jump out for the flags while you unlock the..."

"Forget it--I'm not going Norris...!!!"

The following Saturday afternoon, at 12:29, we were six blocks from the Glenview Naval Air Station, in old man Fester's black Lincoln convertible. It was a beautifully mild sunny day. Too nice a day to die, I thought, as I sat rigidly in the rear of the car, wearing sunglasses and a four-star general's uniform, featuring seven rows of military ribbons.

Norris wheeled our big car skillfully down the suburban streets. Those few people in the neighborhood stared at us with obvious respect. We must have made an impressive sight, starred flags stiffly poised on our gleaming fenders, heralding the importance of the high-ranking "naval" personage within.

"Jesus, here we are!" I called to Fester. I could see there were at least four S.P.'s at the main gate.

"Hey, we're in luck," he observed, "no other cars--coming at mess time was a good idea." He turned into the approach. "Remember, they're enlisted men. Treat 'em like shit."

Two of the Shore Patrol men stepped from their cubicle,

tentatively blocking our way. One of them held a clipboard. My driver slowed only a little, beeping the horn impatiently.

When the S.P.'s realized we weren't going to stop, they jumped back, snapped to attention, and brought their hands up to salute. I returned their salutes perfunctorily as we whizzed by. I managed to look bored while actually being on the point of filling my general's trousers at any moment.

"Did you see the stupid looks on their faces?" asked Norris, laughing. "They nearly crapped in their leggings."

"Let's get out of here!" I shouted, as we turned onto the runway.

"Hell no, we just got in. Besides, don't forget you're the highest ranking officer on the base. The others'll be having shit-fits in a few minutes when they find out you're here."

"But, Norris, my uniform isn't even Navy. They'll know something's wrong for sure when they notice I'm a general."

"Ha Ha, don't worry about it. They'll have to get pretty close to notice the difference. Now, settle back 'Admiral' and enjoy your ride."

We were racing along in front of the control tower and hangars. Fester must have been doing fifty. I watched a Navy transport take off. This place was huge. The row of hangars seemed to have no end.

Suddenly, at the last of the buildings, he braked to a quick stop, and turned off the engine, jumping out to open the rear door for me. I got up as pompously as I could, wondering how often you're allowed to write home from Leavenworth.

Directly in front of the hangar stood two bluejackets with their mouths open in surprise. They each awkwardly held a rifle. Norris, leading the way said something angrily to them. They brought their rifles up to a sloppy "present arms," and I again responded with a demeaning perfunctory salute.

My driver continued on to the smaller door in the hangar covered with red stenciled letters warning, "Keep Out; Restricted, Authorized

Personnel Only." He opened the door for me, then stepped quickly inside closing it behind him. It took our eyes awhile to adjust, having come from the bright sunlight. "Geez, there she is!" exhulted Norris. "Isn't she beautiful?"

But I didn't care about the plane. "What about those guys outside? What did you say to them?"

"Will you stop worrying. I told them you were in from Washington on a snap inspection--and they should see to it the 'Admiral' wasn't disturbed." He climbed on the Shooting-Star's wing. "I also said they looked pitiful and you'd probably have their asses court martialed."

"Oh great, when they find out we're fakes, they'll probably start shooting."

Fester pulled back the plexiglass canopy. "Hey, you should see this cockpit. Man, I've never seen one like this."

I moved closer to the fuselage. "Let's get the hell out of here."

Fester crawled over the edge of the cockpit and disappeared inside. "This is fantastic. Climb up on the wing so you can see these instruments." His voice sounded muffled.

"I'll just appreciate its beauty from outside here. I don't have to get in."

"Aw come on, Admiral." His head popped up. "We're looking at a huge step forward in aircraft design. Look at the configuration of this..." His head disappeared again.

A door at the hangar's rear had suddenly opened and a sailor wearing a pistol-belt entered and snapped on a large overhead light. He blinked in surprise when he saw me. I was a good thirty yards away. "I'm sorry Sir," came his words echoing across the expanse. "I didn't know you were in here." Fester stared at him through the P-80's windscreen.

"That's alright, son." I projected my deepest voice. "We're just doing a little checking in here."

"Yes Sir," he saluted. "Excuse me, Sir." He did an about face and marched out, leaving the light on.

"Oh man, we're in for it now," I yelled at Norris. "He's probably running for the Base Commander."

"Hey, that light sure helps. Get up here and check out this cockpit."

I climbed on the skinny wing, but fear made the aircraft's details swim before my eyes. For some agonizing twenty minutes I urged Fester to leave while he completely ignored me, commenting from time to time on the plane's most impressive characteristics. He even dragged a ladder over so he could gaze into the jet's open nose. "Wow, can you imagine the horsepower this baby develops?"

"Please Norris, you've seen it. Let's get out of here."

"Well, yeh, O.K.," he muttered. He came down the ladder, and began dragging it away.

"Forget the damn lad...."

The rear door popped open again, and a sailor wearing a sidearm stood framed in the sunlight. I couldn't tell if it were the same guy as before.

"Do you have security clearance to be in here?" Fester angrily yelled out.

"Ah, w-w-well s-s-sir," he stammered, trying to adjust his

41

sight to the dully lighted interior. "I uh..."

"Speak up sailor," bellowed Fester.

"Ah, y-yes s-sir, or no sir." He spun out on his heels and slammed the door.

"O.K., let's blow this firetrap," ordered Norris, moving toward the front of the hangar. "Remember to take it easy and treat 'em like shit."

Outside, I quietly, but happily acknowledged the "present arms" of those two apprehensive blue-jackets, while Fester strode purposefully to our car and opened the rear door. No "enemy forces," coming to insure our lengthy vacation in a federal prison, were in sight as yet.

The big Lincoln leaped into motion, and tore down the runway next to the hangars that seemed to stretch on forever. Oh Lord, I thought, this is one helluva big place. We've got a long ways to go.

Suddenly, there were no more thoughts. Just panic. A jeep load of men had turned onto the runway ahead, and was speeding directly toward us. "Watch it Norris, here they come."

"Don't worry, I see 'em. You outrank 'em all Admiral!" His laugh had a nervous edge to it.

As they drew nearer, I could see they wore Shore Patrol insignia. A couple clutched rifles. Moving on a collision course, an officer next to the driver held up his hand in a kind of shaky "stop" signal. Fester tromped down on the accelerator. "Let's play chicken!" he yelled.

I pretended to adjust my sunglasses. Actually, I was considering whether or not to cover my eyes so I couldn't see.

Their jeep swerved aside. Whether they stopped or merely slowed I couldn't tell, we were moving so fast. I did manage a quick salute, though.

We approached the turn leading to the main entrance. My driver swung into it with authority, slowing only a little. I fully expected a fusillade of bullets. Instead, the one S.P. stepped back into the gate house. Apparently, he wasn't going to act alone to stop the Admiral's four-star charger. He saluted smartly. I returned it, and then sagged back into the seat while we roared away.

"Holy Balls," I exclaimed.

"We aren't out of it yet," yelled Fester, "that jeep will be after us."

In the schoolyard, the three girls, attired in very brief shorts and halters, were waiting for us behind the main building. They jumped in the car as we leaped out. Fester dashed to the front for the flags while I fumbled with the trunk. It seemed to take forever to get it open.

Norris tossed the flags in, then pulled his jumper up and his pants off. He threw the whites into a corner of the trunk. "Dammit, what am I going to do with this uniform?" I asked, eyeing his blue shorts and casual tee-shirt.

"Don't worry," he replied, "just hop in."

"You don't mean in there?"

"Yeh, quick, we don't have time for anything else." I climbed in on all fours, but when he closed the trunk, I was flattened, his father's cap crushed over my eyes. I pushed it up, but it was dark in there anyway. "Remember, keep quiet," he instructed.

The car took off fast. To keep from being bounced around like a basketball, I grabbed and clutched for anything. I got the spare tire, and I thought, part of the jack. My hands slid in the grease, but I held on.

A couple of minutes later, we slowed, and I heard some muffled shouts. Fester called out, "No, we didn't see anybody." Then there were a number of wolf-whistles that quickly faded away. I thought, <u>the jeep must have passed us. Wow, that was close.</u>

We seemed to be moving at a reasonable speed. I could tell that Fester and the girls were laughing and talking, but I couldn't make out what they were saying. This confinement began to have a panicky effect on me. I wished my watch had a luminescent dial. I'd lost track of time. Were we out of danger?

The car bounced twice, and I banged my head. We stopped. Norris and the girls laughed. "Fester!" I yelled. I heard a feminine voice, but I couldn't understand the words.

Then Fester said loudly, "Four chocolate shakes, and four hot dogs with everything."

"Norris," I screamed, "get me outta here!" I pounded on the car with my fists. "Damn you, Norris, I want outta here!"

He yelled, "Miss, could make that six shakes, and six hot dogs? The Admiral must be hungry by now."

Sigma Alpha Epsilon is an excellent Fraternity and it was excellent at Northwestern. Their House was right next to ours and built almost to the same configuration.

The fourth floors were directly opposite and someone noticed one of their usually open windows had no screen, and that a single dangling light bulb hung just inside it.

It was a challenge!

On warm Tuesday and Friday nights (not to be too obvious) we'd sneak up to our fourth floor, douse the lights, quietly raise our screen and use an air pellet gun to shoot out the beckoning target.

We got a terrific kick out of popping their bulb, conjecturing on how they must be mystified by the broken glass, and appreciating the efficient replacement of the light.

This sport continued a few weeks until we found our light shattered and a hole through the screen attesting to the velocity of their porjectile. The challenge had been met. The game was over, but it'd been fun while it lasted.

47

When not eating at the training table with one of our athletic teams, I worked a "board-job" in my fraternity house. I helped set up the dining room, waited on tables, or washed dishes. We "board-job" boys were not looked down upon at all by those whom we facetiously referred to as "the rich kids." Positions like ours were much in demand, and we were kind of a "chosen few," we were even envied by some, because of our free and unusually generous meals.

For example, while the multitude in the dining room sat wearing coats and ties, and tried to find choice morsels of fried chicken, we relaxed in our serving jackets licking our lips after consuming the legs and tender breast parts.

"What kind of chickens are these Riordan? They don't have breasts or legs."

"Those are 'racing capons'--you know, males don't have breasts, and their legs are shriveled from all that running. Can I get you gentlemen more wings, or necks?"

48

"Oh yeah, bullshit!"

"Would you like a large or small bowl?"

This type of conversation would take place often, however, always far from Mrs. Joss our respected and revered Housemother.

Only someone seated at one of the back tables would have the temerity to ask, "What are we having tonight, Riordan?"

"Rat shit."

"Well, at least it's something we're used to."

After dessert a couple of steady gripers often pleaded, "We're still hungry, can't you sneak some more food out here?"

I always answered, "There's a candy machine on the second floor."

Actually, the food was great, and everybody ate quite well. Those in the dining room maintained their health and respective weights, while the board-job boys steadily got fatter and fatter.

We picked the choicest morsels and also arranged our own special desserts. If the dessert of the evening turned out to be a chocolate sundae, everyone in the dining room received a medium-sized scoop, anointed with a modest dab of chocolate syrup. In the confines of the kitchen and pantry, we favored few enjoyed soup bowls of ice-cream covered with entire, individual cans of hot fudge.

Some of the rich kids swore they could see us getting pudgier by the day. But they didn't have to clean up, do silverware, wash hundreds of dishes, and scour pots and pans.

We ate magnificently, worked hard and maintained an excellent espirit de corps.

We always left the kitchen together, yelling in unison; our cry of victory and resolve echoing to the highest reaches of the fraternity house. "Our kids are never going to have to suffer like this. Never!!!"

THE VIRGINS' PROTEST

I suppose even if we weren't going to school on a sexless campus, most of us would have been interested in the Kinsey Report. Yes, Doctor Alfred Kinsey, was the first to publish a lucid and in depth account of human sexual behavior.

While most of the "report" though statistical seemed fascinating, to us "starved" fraternity-men, one figure stood out. The average male of our age engaged in two and two-tenths sexual encounters per week.

Although we obviously weren't average, our house was too sophisticated to protest. A fraternity near us, however, facing the main street, Sheridan Road, erected a huge sign. It read:

Kinsey says most guys have
SEX 2.2 times per week
Northwestern girls are unfair.
Our average .000000087
times per week.

We got a big kick out of their declaration, as did everyone who saw it. Some days later a group of the Brothers and I were walking past when one stopped, studied the sign, then turned to us and said, "Hey, there's a mystery for you. How come <u>they're</u> gettin' so much??"

A CHANCEY PROPOSITION

There had to be some way to find out in advance, which campus coeds would be receptive to my romantic overtures - or so I thought during my fifth month at Northwestern University.

I reasoned that a guy of my limited means had to establish a small list of girls who were the proverbial "sure things." I didn't have much money, so I couldn't afford to waste any. My idea of a sure thing, of course, was a coed who would kiss me goodnight on the fourth date.

With this erotic fantasy in mind, I designed a large punch-board with thirty holes in it, each hole covered by a piece of paper with a different number written on it. Above these thirty was a circular piece of paper with the word "PRIZE" printed on it covering the winning number. Nearby was stated, "Winner will not be announced until all <u>chances</u> are sold."

At the top of my board I pasted a large picture of a gaily colored blanket and a photo of an Indian Chief in full-feathered headdress.

Armed with my board, I'd stop pretty girls on campus, introduce myself and smilingly ask the all important question, "How would you like to take a chance on an Indian Blanket?"

Most of the girls were naive and didn't understand. Some did, and let me know immediately, "You're really disgusting."

"You can't be going to school here, you pervert."

But, many coeds did spend a dime, and giggled while I punched out a chance and ceremoniously took their names and phone numbers so I could call them with the good news. I certainly did intend to call them, one way or another.

By the third day I had only one chance left. I sold that to a lovely brunette with violet eyes and sexy voice, "I think you're a devil, but I'll take a chance on your Indian Blanket."

That evening, I decided she had won. When I called her, she said she couldn't wait for me to deliver it. I couldn't either.

All the next day I roamed dreary Chicago discount houses. I'd taken in $3.00, but the best deal I could make on a blanket that looked remotely Indian was $6.95. I figured $3.95 was a fair investment for a torrid relationship with a gorgeous woman.

She seemed somewhat disappointed in the blanket. "Is this authentic Indian? It says made in Japan."

"Well," I said, "I believe we have some sort of cultural exchange program."

"Oh," she replied, "you see it's rather important because my fiance loves Indian things."

"Your fiance?"

"Yes, that's why I took a chance on your Indian Blanket. He's a lawyer in Chicago, I did it for him."

"How nice," I observed reaching for my coat and shaking her hand.

I felt disappointed, but I knew I still had my list of 29 rather warm coeds who had expressed an interest in my Indian Blanket. I called them and leaped into an orgy of dating.

These relationships proved to be extremely educational. In a short period of time I learned about Northwestern women.

Although each one had "taken a chance" none of them would kiss me goodnight, even on the fourth date.

FOR MY BRUSH ALONE

Around 8:00 a.m. every weekday morning the toilet facilities on each floor of my fraternity house were very busy, filled with guys shaving, combing hair, showering and brushing teeth, all in a mad rush to get to 8:30 classes.

Because I had to be frugal, my toothpaste tube always was of the super-large economy size. Chet also used a king-sized tube, so both of ours stood out among all those on the long glass shelf above the wash basins and in front of the mirrors.

For some reason, many of the guys would reach out for my big tube and put a glob of my paste on their tooth-brushes. I knew it wasn't malice or jocularity, rather it probably was the convenience. But also, for some reason, they never used Chet's.

I asked him about the phenomenon. He seemed pleased that I'd noticed. "Oh, they grab yours simply because it's the most conspicuous, and it's there. I keep mine so messy, no one else will ever grab it."

His wisdom amazed me. It didn't take me long to get a bunch of dried paste generously impregnated with my hair cemented securely around the opening nozzle of my toothpaste tube. It looked grungy.

And, miracle of miracles -- the Brothers would reach for it, stop, and after contemplation grab their own. No one else used my toothpaste anymore excepting, of course -- Chet.

SUNK BY THE QUEEN

There's a collegiate song that states, Northwestern is noted for its beautiful girls. I'd have to agree. Our school abounded with lovelies, and our campus boasted numerous "beauty queens," such as the Navy Ball Queen, Syllabus Queen, Big Ten Queen, Rose Bowl Queen and a lot of others. It was a notable accomplishment, of course, to date one of these queens, even though the "untitled girls" were plenty good enough.

One Saturday evening Cleveland Garrison III, our social chairman, came into my room reeking of beer and onions. He didn't live in the fraternity house, so he had eaten elsewhere.

"Guess who I've got a date with tonight?" he asked, plopping into my battered easy chair.

"One of the nurses at Evanston Hospital," I answered, somewhat annoyed by his odor.

"No, Candace Bonanza, the fair queen of the "sailor testicle!"

I'll have to admit I was impressed and a little surprised.

Garrison didn't seem her type even though his father was a multi-millionaire. "Gee, the Navy Ball Queen, she's really gorgeous."

"I knew you'd want to congratulate me on my good taste. But I have to admit I actually stopped in your dismal quarters to borrow one of your ties."

"Take your pick," I said, flicking a thumb at my tie rack. "Listen Cleveland, (he insisted on being called "Cleveland"), you can't go out with a breath like that, you'll peel paint."

He picked out a blue-knit, "Is it that bad? I had a couple of hamburgers with bermuda onions at Hackney's"

"She'll get a whiff of you and run back upstairs. I can hardly stand you myself."

He looked around my room. "Well, what do you have for bad breath?"

"I never need anything. My breath is always like rosebuds."

"Hey how about this," he said, moving to my dresser and picking up the super large bottle of Old Spice I'd recently received for my birthday. "It smells good."

"No dice Cleveland, that's shaving lotion."

"Well, it might work." With that hopeful supposition, he chugged down the entire bottle, hardly pausing for a breath.

"Why you dizzy---"

"How's it now?" He exhaled powerfully in my direction.

I almost fainted. "It's worse that an outhouse."

He tossed my empty Old Spice bottle in the wastebasket. "I don't want to be late. I've got a date with a Queen," he declared confidently as he strode out.

About an hour later he returned, looking quite dejected. "You were right. She said 'not in your condition' and went back upstairs. Then the Housemother kicked me out."

"What did you expect?" I chuckled, "she's a Queen."

"Gee, I feel rotten," he said, "I need a drink. You got something to drink around here?"

"Not a damn thing," I replied, attempting to hide my bottle of Aqua Velva.

BETTER THAN A SEAMSTRESS

A number of us were going to the Delta Gamma Sorority Formal and I was doubling with Brad. About an hour before we were to leave, Brad spilled some hot cigarette ashes on his tuxedo trousers in the area of the crotch. Before he could extinguish them, a pattern of holes had burned through.

"What am I going to do? Do you have a needle and thread?" He asked me.

"Are you kidding?" I replied, laughing. "Even if I did, I couldn't do anything."

In desperation, Brad went up and down the halls of our House yelling "Does anyone have needle and thread? Do any of you guys know how to sew?"

Mostly he was greeted with hoots of laughter. Even the WW II vets didn't know how to sew. "Better wear your cords," some wise guy called out.

Even our wonderful Housemother Mrs. Joss was at a loss for the immediate moment. "It's going to take some careful darning at least and we don't have the time for it now."

"Maybe you could pull the jacket down lower," I ventured rather foolishly.

"No, that wouldn't work," said Brad, looking in a full length mirror. "It really shows. I'll just have to cancel out."

At that moment, in walked the intrepid Norris Fester, nattily attired in formal wear. We explained the problem to him.

"No problem," he said.

He directed Brad to take his pants off and follow him. We both did, until he found a Brother with a bottle of black ink. He poured some of it over the front of Brad's shorts.

Brad howled, "You could have at least waited until I got them off Norris."

Fester merely smiled at a job well done. Over the dryed shorts, the burn holes didn't show at all.

"Gee thanks, Norris," said Brad. "Say, how come you're so smart?"

Fester sighed as his gaze swept the room. "Superior intelligence always triumphs over common stupidity."

Quite a few students who lived on campus had cars. I never owned one, but I usually managed to have close access to wheels.

Our beautiful campus ran for about a mile along Lake Michigan with the mens' housing quadrangles on the north and womens' housing quadrangles on the south. Rumor had it the University planned it that way to keep the sexes apart. Anyway, a car wasn't necessary for on campus activity, but when it came to dating, partying, or going to Chicago, efficient transportation could be very handy.

Parking in the mens' area was quite abundant, however, finding a spot around the south quads was much more difficult. This led my fertile mind into conversations like the following:

"Gee, Justine, there doesn't seem to be any place to park. There's that small place over there, but I think it's too small for a car of this size."

"Lee darling, why don't we snuggle for a few minutes, and then you take the car up north and bring it back, whenever."

I'd look bewildered, "Gee Justine -- if you think that's O.K. -- Well, O.K."

Or another effective scenario would be: "Cloris, we've got a date Wednesday night and next Saturday, too. Why don't I take the car so you won't be bothered with it?

"Oh Lee, would you do that for me?"

"Why sure Cloris. I'd be glad to."

The beautiful coeds avoided any even subtle hints about sexual contact, but they often did have big, gorgeous automobiles. Many times after I'd drop my date off by the mandatory 2:00 a.m., I'd head for Chicago's Outer Drive and race down it with the radio blaring and the top down. Oh, what joy; what rapture!

One afternoon a couple of my fraternity brothers asked if I'd drive them into Chicago. "We know you've got the wheels Riordan." One of them stated.

I wasn't busy at the time, so I said, "Sure guys, be glad to."

Out in our lake front parking lot there stood three cars in a row, all available to me, a yellow Cadillac convertible; a Chrysler Town and Country convertible with wood grained exterior panels; and a green Dodge four door.

"How come you accepted the Dodge sedan?" asked one of the brothers.

I thought a moment. "The young lady with the green Dodge has a terrific personality."

DINING WITH MARCUS ANTONIUS

"You're too big for a spear carrier," announced David the director, handing me a short sword and a huge Roman helmet. "You'll be an officer." A large group of us were on the sandy shores of Lake Michigan shooting Northwestern's film version of Julius Caesar, starring a grad student named Charlton Heston as Mark Antony.

Although it took lots of time, making the movie was fascinating and all the actors, especially Heston were excellent. I was happy to be part of the production, particularly in the role of an officer. Yes, even though my part was small and non-speaking, to be an officer must be better than a spear carrier.

With all the film locked away "in the can," we celebrated with several cast parties. One took place on the beach, featuring steak sandwiches.

I walked barefoot through the sand carrying a coke and sandwich and sat down next to "Mark Antony." He greeted his admirers eating

"homemade peanut butter and jelly."
He had a goodly supply of double-deckers, cut in half, beside him.

He must have noticed my questioning look because he said, "Peanut butter and jelly is the best sandwich in the world." Then he handed me one that was carefully wrapped.

I compared the two sandwiches taking a bite from the steak first and then Heston's peanut butter and jelly.

Darned if he wasn't right.

The peanut butter and jelly <u>was</u> definitely tastier.

A COUSIN FOR "LUNCH"

My fraternity brother Norris Fester, with whom I was very close, was a "Townie." This simply meant he did not live in the Fraternity House, but with his folks -- in his case, the nearby suburb of Winnetka.

There once was a popular song entitled "The Big Noise From Winnetka," written about Fester, I felt always certain.

His folks kept up a lovely home, and I spent many delightful hours even some overnights there. General Fester, Norris's dad, traveled quite a bit, and his mother often went along. It was a nice setup for me, and while Fester often got me in trouble, I liked and admired him a great deal.

One Sunday evening, after a particularly close game of ping-pong, we sat down with a soda and Fester told me about a problem. "This Friday my rotten cousin Ted from New York arrives for the weekend."

"Don't you like him at all?" I asked.

"I've always wanted to kill him," replied Norris vehemently. "I hate the son of a bitch."

"Gee, what are you going to do?"

He took a long drink of root-beer. I'm going to fix it so his guts are scared shitless, and you're going to help me."

Now, it was my turn to take a long draft of root-beer. "How?" I questioned meekly.

"We'll use the dogs!"

Fester had two of the biggest black Labradors I'd ever seen "Tiger Attack" and "Linda." Linda was the female. For years, I'd been afraid of dogs, but this pair had always been gentle to me. Fester considered them to be two of the most ferocious monsters in Chicago's North Shore area. He usually secured them on stout chains.

All week long, he kept talking vaguely about his plan to have his hated cousin "scared shitless."

On Saturday evening at the house, with Fester's folks away as usual, the plan unfolded. My friend Norris was shaking with glee.

"How's Ted?" I stupidly asked.

"He's in one piece, but only for a few more hours. When he comes back, Tiger Attack and Linda are going to go after him."

Both dogs growled. Fester grinned in satisfaction.

"Where is he?"

"He went to Chicago. I told him to get back by midnight."

"So what's the plan?" I asked leaning back on the sofa.

"It's simple but deadly!" Fester grinned again and handed me a root-beer. "He thinks I gave him the key to the house, but I gave him another one that won't work. When he can't get in he'll try the porch windows and I'll leave one slightly open. He'll crawl in, right on top of Tiger Attack and Linda who I'll have sleeping under it."

"As you said," I observed holding back my feelings of apprehension, "the plan's simple enough."

"I haven't fed them for a couple of days. These two dogs will really go after him." Norris clapped his hands with anticipation. Both dogs barked and jumped with belligerence.

About 11:30 that evening, he decided it was time for us to get in position, "in case that dumb bastard comes early." We sat on the rug of a room adjoining the one with the slightly open window. Tiger Attack and Linda were getting settled beneath it. All lights in the house had been extinguished. The four of us were in the dark.

At 12:30, Fester checked his luminous watch and announced: "It's twelve-thirty. Where is that deadbeat?"

At 1:00 a.m. he announced: "It's one a.m. Where is that deadbeat?" I had dozed off. "Hey, Lee don't go to sleep on me. You might miss the fun."

Perhaps, that had been my intention. I wasn't sure.

Around 1:20 Ted arrived. We went on immediate alert. Both dogs were in place sleeping, one actually snoring.

The cousin did exactly as Fester had planned. He fumbled with the lock trying to open the front door, cursing generously. This lasted for about five minutes, then he went down the stairs and onto the walk.

"Dammit," said Norris. We couldn't see outside from our room.

In a few minutes, however, Ted was back working at the front door. Again, he cursed at his failure. We could hear him humming between expletives. He seemed drunk. For awhile he remained outside the door humming. Soon he began walking around the front porch.

"The window dummy," whispered Fester. "The window!"

Immediately we could hear him fumbling at a locked window. He struggled with it, but, of course, it wouldn't open. The he moved across the porch, stopped humming and gripped <u>the</u> window. With a squeal of protest, it opened up all the way.

Fester grabbed my arm and pulled me so that we both could see into the darkened front room. "Here's where he's lunch meat," whispered my buddy.

Pushing the curtains aside, and still humming a happy tune, Ted stuck one foot through the window, followed by the other, which must have touched one of the dogs because there came an abbreviated bark and a short growl.

Now, standing full in the room Ted stopped humming and softly repeated "Nice doggie, nice doggie." In the dark he got to the stairs and climbed them to the second floor where he turned on a light. It illuminated the dogs both still sleeping peacefully.

Fester handed me a root beer, took one himself and drank a huge gulp. Then he stepped in the room where the dogs lay. Instantly, they jumped up on him barking and growling.

"Down Tiger! Down Linda!" They dropped whimpering before him.

"What happened, Norris?" I asked bewildered.

"I dunno. Maybe I should've fed 'em"

"Well, what do we do now?"

Fester snapped on the light and drank root beer thoughtfully. "I'm not sure, but it's definitely back to the drawing board."

"SOUTH QUAD MAN"

Comic books were quite popular during the time I was in school, and while we Northwestern intellectuals didn't read them, most of us were at least vaguely familiar with "Batman," and "Spiderman," and a few of the others. With the encouragement of some of my Fraternity Brothers, to prove myself as a "pledge," I became "South Quad Man" -- a black-clad male animal who "terrified" the women's residences.

Actually, it was more of a joke. The girls loved to see my form streaking by, and often shouted terms of endearment toward me. I always wore a tight black sweat suit with close-fitted hood. My hands and face were blackened, and ebony sneakers completed my outfit. It was a point of honor never to sneak up on couples who were necking. Besides, I might antagonize some sprinter on the track team who would run me down. Generally, I appeared quickly, and disappeared just as rapidly. Now, and then, on the campus, I overheard girls talking about me. Yes, I was indeed the legendary South Quad Man.

One especially daring night -- my last excursion although I didn't know it at the time -- I decided to climb the fire-escape at Willard Hall, the Freshman Girl's Dorm. I was very athletic so had little difficulty scampering up to the third floor. I peered in some of the windows on the way, but didn't see anything thrilling.

The hour was late. The girls were eating chocolate chip cookies and drinking milk when one spotted me perched on the ledge. They screeched and shouted more out of delight than fear. They kept asking who I really was, and insisted I eat some milk and cookies. "Do you go to school here?'

I answered that I attended only "night" classes. They seemed to think that was pretty funny. Many of the windows were open with girls staring, and some had removed screens and were leaning out.

"Why don't you come in?"

"Why don't you spend the night, we'll hide you."

I considered staying while munching more cookies and milk. Some of those nighties were pretty cute, but I knew I'd be cutting off my escape route. Besides, I liked it at Northwestern.

Suddenly, some "crazy" on the second floor started shouting. "Help me, oh help me!" the voice wailed. No one could accuse that particular young lady of not having a sense of humor. But, the joke was over. "Help me!," she screamed.

I figured I better leave, and bounded down the fire escape. As I swung to the sidewalk, I almost bumped into the night-watchman. He yelled something at me in a foreign language and began unlimbering his gun. I took off streaking past ZTA Sorority and zig-zagged out into the open quad. Although running as fast as I could, I kept waiting for the shot.

It came.

Later on when some girls talked about the incident to me, I pretended to be shocked. "Must have been some kind of pervert," I observed. "Well, I could see the

night-watchman," said one, "I saw
him shoot in the air."
    I thought, _whatever_ -- I _know_ _he_
missed.

You could tell by the drooping "Exam Week Is Hell" banner on our House that part of the week had passed. Actually it was Tuesday night. By now everyone had taken at least one final, probably two, and almost certainly faced the prospect of a couple more.

Nerves were frayed and tempers short; eyes beginning to blear from inadequate sleep. Some guys wore "lucky" sweatshirts and didn't bathe and nobody shaved. It was generally considered unlucky to shave.

As in world affairs, at times small, insignificant occurrences can develop into momentous, never-to-be-forgotten events. One of those seemingly insignificant occurrences; because of the high level of tension, happened in our House that Tuesday night.

Miles and Dan were roommates on the third floor. Miles headed for the toilet facilities carrying a book. Dan called out, "Where are you going with that Econ Book?"

"I'm going to read it on the john," Miles yelled toward their room.

"Well, I need it!" shouted Dan.

"You'll have it in a little while."

This reply evidently angered Dan. He called out "While you're in there, you better take a shower too. You smell like a horse barn."

Now, this evidently angered Miles, who stopped in the hall and shouted, "What did you say, Dan?"

"I said Miles, that you stink like a horse barn!"

"Well you can stuff it!" yelled Miles. "I'm dropping the Econ book in the john."

That must've been it for Dan, his breaking point. He ran out into the hall glaring at Miles, who was about twenty feet away. "You stink so much I'm going to wash you myself." Then he opened the glass and steel box holding the fire hose, and unwound it.

A couple of Brothers watched incredulous. So did Miles.

Dan spun the red wheel next to the hose box. Quickly, the fire-hose became a "living" thing. A watery blast caught Miles in the chest and knocked him backward.

There was so much pressure that a Brother coming up the stairs tumbled in the wash, regained his feet cursing, ran to the fourth floor and unlimbered the fire-hose there.

Now, as in world affairs, the insignificant occurrence was about to become a momentous, never-to-be-forgotten event. It probably never would have happened if it hadn't been the middle of exam week. But, there were stated excuses by historians for the World Wars, too.

Soon each fire-hose in our House belched under full pressure. Every occupant was involved except our Housemother. Oh, some of the officers tried at first to stop it, however, they were quickly swept away in one of the many torrents. It was beyond description, absolutely complete chaos.

There were men manning hoses against other men manning hoses. Guys looked like ten-pins knocked down by powerful streams. Bodies flipped in the air or slid down the halls as the water deepened. Nobody thought about exams in the complete aqueous orgy. Giggling and laughing insanely, nobody wanted to stop.

I was swept down the stairs from the second floor by a veritable Niagara Falls. At least a foot of water covered the front hall and living room, and still it came.

Some wise guys had put our canoe in the front hall complete with paddle and then crawled upstairs into the real action. I checked with our Housemother in her flooded first floor apartment, via the canoe, to see if she were O.K.

Although a couple of lights had shorted out, and she stood atop a sofa, she was fine, if somewhat chagrined. "I've never seen anything like this," she said. In all my years here, I've never seen anything like this."

Then she smiled and said, "Lee, would you paddle me over to that blue sofa in the living room? I think I left my needle point there." I maneuvered close to her vantage point, and she jumped in. It took some careful work and substantial effort. After all, I'd never paddled a canoe in a living room before. We avoided a floating coffee table and retrieved her needle point.

I paddled back to her apartment and dropped her off. When I got back into the hall, the water level had dropped and my canoe bottomed.

By the sound of things, everyone had quieted down upstairs, and the fire hoses had been shut off. Plenty of water still poured down the stairs, including bits of flotsam and jetsam, and a battered book.

I picked up the completely soaked volume gingerly so it wouldn't fall apart. The title was hardly decipherable but I recognized it instantly as an Econ book.

COLD COMBAT

The "Little Esquire" was Evanston's premier ice cream store, no fancy trappings and no fast food, just incomparable orchestrations in ice cream. When it came to floats, shakes, sundaes, malts, splits or ice cream sodas, N.U. students knew the "Esquire" had no peers.

When you ordered a malt you got the usual tall glass, then they handed you the mixing container upside down. Yes, so thick was the delicious mixture that mere gravity had no effect on it. You had to bump and knock it in to your glass. Straws simply crumpled if you tried to insert them.

The "Little Esquire" had a standing offer -- drink two of their malts, and all subsequent ones were on the house. With my healthy appetite, and six-foot 220 pound frame, I figured I was a promising candidate for at least one free malt. But, when it came to performing in the ice cream shop, the malts were so huge and thick, I found try as I would, I never could quite finish the second one. It was simply too much for me.

By contrast, my Fraternity brother Bernie, a 265 pound football defensive lineman, easily downed three, always enjoying his free third malt with special gusto. He usually claimed he had room for more, however, he never demolished more than three at one sitting.

"Three malts" made Bernie a legend in our House. His prowess was well known, and no one disputed his superiority except Norris Fester. Norris flatly stated that he could drink more L.E. malteds than anyone in our Fraternity -- he expanded his statement to include the entire University -- and he issued a challenge to Bernie specifically.

"He's got to be out of his cotton-picking head," was a typical reaction to Fester's threat of encroachment on Bernie's kingdom. We all knew him as a torrid competitor, but Norris stood about five nine and weighed 160 pounds wearing heavy shoes. He'd be outweighed by over 100 pounds.

Of course, the prospect of a competition between these two

evolved quite naturally. "They're both such nice guys, I'd hate to see either one of them hurt," opined one of the Brothers. Alas, a time and the usual place were set, a Friday night two weeks away, at 8:00 o'clock so their dinners would have settled a bit. I couldn't imagine them eating at all before the confrontation.

I never was a betting man, probably because I couldn't afford to be, however I'd seen Fester eat a number of times, and I put all my spare cash on him to win. There were plenty of guys to bet with at five and even ten to one. "Glad to take your money, Lee. But, it's a shame you're so gullible." It was true that Bernie could wrap his arms around Norris and virtually make him disappear.

The night of the "contest" found the Little Esquire packed. Many men and women students stood on the steps and overflowed into the street. The contestants were seated opposite each other across a table. Bernie wore his purple letter sweater, and Fester was attired in a white shirt with the tails hanging out. I held Norris's coat and car keys in case he wouldn't be able to drive at the end. A two hour limit was set, they wished each other luck, and the contest began with a chorus of cheers.

Bernie downed the first malt quickly, somewhat ahead of Fester who seemed to be biding his time. The second took longer for both, Bernie laughing and joking while Norris drank slowly, apparently in deep concentration. Midway through the third, Bernie's face began to redden, and he slowed his pace, but still finished ahead of his opponent accompanied by rousing cheers. The issue here, however, was not speed but volume. While waiting for Norris to down the "third," I noticed the white "N" on Bernie's sweater had become distorted.

They both took some time staring at number four, neither one eager to begin. The huge football player's face seemed a slash of crimson while his much smaller opponent remained implacably unchanged. All those in the audience held their collective breaths while the gladiators ingested malt four. It must have been like swallowing sweetened cement. Each sip took minutes.

Gradually, the letter on Bernie's sweater looked less and less like an "N" and more and more like a "Z." He was breathing heavily. Some of his closest fans helped him out of his sweater to cool his perspiration. He and Norris finished number four in a dead heat.

Someone yelled out, "Is there a Doctor in the house?," as number five appeared before the combatants. When they reached for their respective malts everyone in the audience applauded. On continued the competition. My many bets seemed definitely in jeopardy. I started to sweat almost as much as Bernie. I certainly could not afford to lose that money.

About midway through malt number five a salient happening took place. Bernie struggled to his feet -- it seemed everything above his belt sagged -- he reached across the table and shook Fester's hand, picked up his sweater and accompanied by his closest buddies and applause staggered for the door. Norris finished his "fifth" to tumultuous cheering.

As he sat there grinning a reporter from our School newspaper, The Daily Northwestern asked him for a comment. Norris thought for a moment, then said quietly to everyone's astonishment, "I think I'll have another."

When he finished his sixth monstrous malt, he quipped. "I wish this place had hamburgers."

After the hero-worship and accolades died down, I drove him home and I spent the night at the Fester house. The next morning he seemed fine and said, "Man, I'm really hungry." Of course, I had seen him eat before, however, this morning he enjoyed his <u>usual</u> breakfast: six eggs, half-a-pound of bacon, a huge helping of hash-browns, five pieces of toast loaded with jam, three glasses of orange juice, and a quart of milk.

I sat opposite him consuming less than a fourth of what he was eating. He looked a bit disturbed and said, "Hey Lee, would you make a couple more pieces of toast? For some reason, this morning I'm really starved!"

The days when football players were known by bona fide nicknames are pretty much in the past. I think the game may have lost some of its spirit when these laurels disappeared. Only the better players were given them and they were a definite mark of distinction. They had to be earned in bloody combat.

I stood a little over six feet and weighed around 195 pounds. Our program listed me as 6-2, 225. Inflating the size of your team members, was common practice in trying to intimidate the opposition. It looked more impressive to the other teams, or so went the theory, anyway.

On offense, I lined up at left-guard. I performed well at that position. I did like to hit. In fact I enjoyed slamming into people on the gridiron.

Ohio State and Michigan did not inflate the heights and weights of their players. They didn't have to. When the Buckeyes stated their All American Defensive Tackle "Bulldog" was six-feet eight inches, and 278 pounds, they weren't kidding. They meant exactly what they said, two-hundred seventy-eight pounds of Ohio State muscle, bone and sinew.

Those guys wearing scarlet and grey were always kind of special to me, for at least a couple of reasons. One, I felt sure they were inspired to do well. None of them wanted to end up working in any Ohio steel-mill or mine, like their Fathers. And two, they had just eaten their Mothers for breakfast.

The week before the Ohio State game, I seldom got any sleep, and my studies slid behind. This particular year I hardly ate for six days. Bulldog was certain to be among those nice boys I'd bump into Saturday afternoon.

Of course, this would be an important confrontation for both teams. It always was, each year, but now we had a chance at the Rose Bowl. There were some real serious practices.

Our coaches even put in an unusually large number of new plays. One of these was "46 Stutter Trap." There are many different formations and plays, but on offense seven men are always lined up front on the line of scrimmage with four backfield men arrayed behind them. The number of the play denotes which "back" will carry the ball and which hole will be opened in the line for him to charge through. The "46 stutter" was a "trap" play. I was to turn to the outside and bump Bulldog, who would have penetrated into our backfield. I would be "trapping" him away from the play, so that "Flatfoot," our halfback could race through the hole where "Mr. All American" had just been.

In practice, our 46 play got nowhere. Our defensive tackles, though not All Americans, were strong and tough, and hard as I tried I couldn't seem to make the block. Each time we ran it, Flatfoot, who could pivot on a dime, and give you change, got crunched. Our coaches screamed at me. "What are you going to do against Bulldog on Saturday, Riordan?" I hated to think. All I could do was pray 46 stutter trap wouldn't be called.

When the day arrived, I had a worse case of diarrhea than usual.

The tension before a game, and there's actually nothing game-like about big time college football, is always rough. Today, it was crushing. Most guys simply up-chuck a few times. With me, it never failed to be the other end. I drank deeply from the cans of stomach-soothing stuff generously dispersed around the dressing room.

During the pre-game drills, I tried not to steal a look at the Buckeyes, but I couldn't avoid spotting Bulldog. Even among those monsters, he stood out. He must have unnerved me a little, because I ran into an OSU band member, knocked him down, cracked his glasses and bent his horn. I didn't apologize, it _was_ a good block. Besides, I needed to get back under the stadium to use the can.

It turned out to be a hell of a conflict. We Wildcats did pretty well. When I came up against Bulldog, I gave him enough to handle. Oh he bashed me on the side of my head and across my Adam's apple with fists as big as catcher's mitts. I bled a lot, but they were only superficial wounds. He hadn't conquered me. So far anyhow, we hadn't used that darn play.

Mid-way through the fourth-quarter we were down by only four points. However, we faced a crucial situation, third and seven on our own thirty-eight. It had to be a pass, we needed seven big yards in one play.

Our quarterback, face bloodied, calmly squatted in our huddle and said, "Forty-six Stutter Trap on four, got it, on Four!"

I thought, he must be nuts. "Center," he ordered, and the center turned and ran up to the waiting ball. "Team," he crackled. We clapped our hands and trotted toward our respective positions at the line.

Sure, I thought, _They won't be expecting us to attack their strength...it hadn't worked in practice...I'd never made the block effectively...against Bulldog at six-eight...why he could reach right over me and cream our ball-carrier._

"Shift," yelled our quarterback. We split out smartly in unison to our "Stutter" formation. "Go," he shouted.

"Kill the sons of bitches," roared a Buckeye linebacker.

"Go!"

One linebacker began dropping back, expecting a pass.

"Go."

Oh God, I thought.

"Go! Go!"

At the instant of the fourth "go," I pivoted both feet left. I kept low, digging for speed and power. Our left-tackle shot ahead to take one of their linebackers. Bulldog penetrated our line, unopposed. Like any good defensive-tackle, he instantly knew since he hadn't been blocked, it must be a trap.

He loomed up like Mount Everest in front of me, half crouched, his massive arms extended eagerly like bludgeons. I aimed my helmet between his legs and drove with everything I had. I kept driving. He grunted as he rode my neck, while the sounds of football combat exploded around us.

We crashed in a heap. I felt the roar of the crowd increasing until it became a single living entity. We leaped to our feet and loped down the field. "Aw shit," Bulldog yelled and slammed me in the back of the helmet.

I hardly noticed. Flatfoot had gone sixty-two yards for a touchdown without a grisly Ohio State hand touching him. Our defense choked them off, and we won.

Later, that evening, Richie the other guard and I were enjoying a sundae in the Sargent Hall cafeteria. We were still wearing our dark purple blazers which were mandatory after any game. A small bunch of students stopped by, and expressed their opinion that it had been quite a contest. We, of course, admitted it had.

Then one fellow, with a massive case of blotchy acne, weighing about 135 pounds, sang out, "Did you guys see Flatfoot's run? Sixty-two yards! He's the whole damn team!"

You might suppose a guy named "Okie" would be from Oklahoma, but he was from Kansas and a quick and imaginative student. He liked to tell how everyone thought he was a Sooner when they learned his name, and brag about how he got his sexual kicks on our campus, while the rest of us could only dream about them.

When he went to Deering Library to study, Okie always wore his personally designed "library shoes." These were fairly heavy and ankle high, with a carefully arrayed series of mirrored prisms affixed to each toe. Each prism was as wide as the shoe, and Okie claimed he could see up the skirt of any girl he sat across from at the study tables.

Many of us had our doubts, however Okie spent every evening in the library and seemed to be having an awful lot of fun. He'd sit opposite one pretty girl for awhile, a big grin on his face, and then move across from another. Most girls wore skirts, so he'd move around quite a bit before the library closed. Darn if he wasn't affecting our study habits. We'd watch _him_ rather than read our textbooks.

Of course, that was long before the "raunch" magazines appeared. A picture of a nicely endowed gal in a modest bathing suit was considered terribly exciting. A photo of a nude woman was about as rare as sex at Northwestern. Anyway, I never saw one even as a so called "pin-up."

Okie told us in graphic detail about the magnificent wonders he was observing, and said confidentially we'd be surprised how many of those gorgeous coeds wore nothing at all under their skirts.

He was driving us sex-starved fraternity-men out of our minds. In a kind of self-defense, some chose to deride him and cast doubt on his stories. Many claimed he couldn't see anything.

This hurt Okie's pride. He was a Science Major and he insisted his prismatic system really worked. "Prove it Okie," some of us jeered. "Prove it."

"O.K. damn it," he answered with grim determination. "I will!"

We watched him operate in the library even more avidly. A week went by, and nothing happened. Around the house he seemed morose, so we knew he was hatching some sort of ingenious plan. He was no dummy.

The following Wednesday night, I spotted him seated across from Northwesterns "Navy Ball" Queen. She looked beautiful and Okie certainly was concentrating. I couldn't take my eyes off them. Suddenly, the reading room blazed with a huge flash.

Students jumped to their feet and Miss Navy Ball started yelling. Quickly, two librarians moved to confront Okie, who frantically tore at a camera attached to his right toe, and a flash device attached to his left.

The picture was fantastic! He'd been telling the truth. That evening at least, the Navy Ball Queen of Northwestern University had not been wearing panties. Over a hundred enlargements were made, many three by five. I mean three by five feet, not inches. Wallet-sized copies were turned out in large numbers so each member of our house could possess at least one. We did not share this photographic masterpiece with anyone outside our group. It was too precious. Besides the lady might be offended.

What happened to Okie you ask? Well, apparently the Administration couldn't figure out exactly what he'd been doing. If they had, I'm sure he would have been banned from the University. He did draw a suspension for a quarter, during which he became interested in medicine.

He's now a very successful gynecologist, not in Kansas, but in Oklahoma.

GIVING BILL A CHARGE

Bill Wagonstern was the only guy in our house who slept under an electric blanket. They were a rather new product in those days, and most of us were rather suspicious of their safety. Would a short circuit fry a person in bed like a piece of toast? What if the blanket with all those wires in it got wet?

Some guys were somewhat envious of Bill - known to everyone as Waggie - and he enjoyed catering to their envy.

"Those blankets are too expensive, Waggie."

"Yes, it does cost a lot, but it's worth every penny."

"Well, what's so great about it?"

"It's so light," answered Waggie, "you hardly know anything is on you. And, the warmth is evenly distributed. You can set it at any temperature you want."

"Yeh, but what if it should get wet? You'd be electrocuted."

Waggie grinned confidently, "Not a chance. It's completely waterproof."

A few nights later four of the fellows who had been discussing Waggie's special blanket with him returned to the house about 11:30 p.m. They'd obviously had a few beers. When they passed my room, I asked, "Hey, what are you guys up to with that bucket?"

"We're going to scare the crap out of Wagonstern and pour water on his electric blanket." They knew he'd be asleep because he had a habit of going to bed early, and sleeping soundly.

"Aw come on guys," I yelled, "leave him alone." They laughed and giggled in reply.

I was taking a photo-journalism course, and I thought this might make a good picture. So, I grabbed my camera and followed them.

They stood around Waggie's bunk swinging the slopping bucket. I was in the corner of the room out of their sight aiming my camera. "Here it comes, Waggie. Let's see if it's waterproof."

As they hurled the water, I punched my camera. The flashbulb exploded in brilliant light and smoke.

The four culprits reacted almost as one.

"Oh, no, we've killed him."

"Waggie, I'm sorry. I didn't mean it."

"He's frying!"

"Get him out of there."

While one kneeled at the bedside praying, the other three tried to pull Waggie out of what they supposed was his electrically charged sack.

"Get his arms."

"Pull him straight out!"

"He's cooking in there!"

Waggie was a heavyweight wrestler and he didn't appreciate being disturbed. He beat the guys away no doubt thinking it was a bad dream. "Leave me alone, I'm sleeping you jerks. Get outta here!"

I pulled the plug for the blanket and lifted the prayerful penitent to his feet. "It was my camera guys. The flashbulb exploded." The jokers shuffled into the hall. I started to follow them.

Waggie, still mostly asleep, called out, "Is that you, Lee?"

"Yeh."

"What's going on?"

"Nothing, go back to sleep."

"There's some water on my face."

"Aw, it's raining. The roof leaks a little."

"Sure, sure - that must be it." He began to snore.

Out in the hall, the others were unhappy with me. "Dammit Riordan you fouled up the whole gag."

"Yeh, Riordan, you just don't have any sense of humor."

"Well, just you jokers remember to mention me in your prayers."

They grumbled as they moved down the hall kicking their empty pail.

I was checking my camera when Waggie called out, "Hey, Lee, could you see if my blanket's plugged in. I feel sort of cold."

I replaced the plug.

"You know I just had a nightmare - you pulled it out."

"Not a chance," I replied, "just a dream."

He rolled over and grunted, "You oughta get one of these blankets. They're really fun."

"Yeh, well, I just might do that - but, after --" then I stopped. Waggie had begun to snore again.

Justine let me use her Cadillac
convertible ostensibly because
parking was readily available up
north around the men's quadrangles
and woefully inadequate down south
around the women's quads. It was
a nice arrangement for me, and I
attributed at least part of the
situation to my charm and rugged
good looks.

Two years of physical education
was required of non-athletes and
Patten Gym, where the P.E. classes
convened stood right behind my
fraternity house. "Patten" fronted
on Sheridan Road, the main North-
South campus street.

At twenty-five minutes after the
hour many students who had just
partaken of gym hitchhiked on
Sheridan Road, going south. There
always were many freshly showered
coeds, who were only too eager to
plop into "my" convertible
especially when the top was down.
What a nice way to make friends.

On this particular day, seven
beauties hopped into the car.
Everyone got along quite amiably

and we traveled about a mile swiftly until forced to stop at a red light next to the Union, Scott Hall.

Justine crossed in front of her car without a sign of recognition. "Hi Justine," I called as the girls piled out murmuring their thanks. "Hi Justine," I yelled this time and honked the horn. She just kept walking.

Later she telephoned me, and began, "Lee, I've been looking for a parking place...."

I interrupted. "I was driving down south to see you."

"You know I've got a 10:30 class."

I could see those wheels rolling away. "I simply picked up hitchhikers in front of Patten."

"Lee, I've been....."

"Justine, I called to you. I blew the horn. The light changed and I had to drive it."

"Lee, would you please let me speak?"

"Sure Justine, shoot." I immediately realized I'd used the wrong verb.

"Lee, I've been looking for a parking place and now I've found one. Please bring my car back."

"O.K.," I said with resignation. "How about tonight at eight?"

"I'd prefer it this afternoon."

"O.K., I'll bring it right down."

In a few minutes I turned over the keys to her at her sorority house. After a few strained words I pointed out that I'd found a parking spot right outside.

"Thank you," she said extending her hand.

"Aren't you going to drive me up north?"

She smiled devilishly, "Why should I? You've found such a perfect parking place."

So, I started walking north. Heck, I thought. _It's only a mile and I'm in terrific shape._

But as I walked, I began to mull over things, generally. It really was going to be a tough, long mile.

So long, Justine.

Goodbye sharp black top.

Goodbye big, impressive yellow car.

So long red leather seats.

But, I still had Cloris's car. I almost escaped from my nostalgia. Cloris's "Town and Country" was really sharp!

"Riordan! Hey, Lee!" A guy called up from the second floor.

I opened the door to my room and yelled, "Yeh, who wants Riordan?"

"You've got a phone on two."

The two main phones were on the first floor, and one of these had an extension on the second, the other on the third.

"O.K., I'll be right there." I was wearing only my undershorts, this warm evening. When I got to the booth, the phone seemed dead. No one was on the line. I tried to find the guy on phone duty but to no avail. Muttering to myself, I began climbing the stairs back to three, and had almost made it when a cargo net dropped over me.

The heavy net made me lose my footing, though it did cushion my fall as I rolled down a few stairs. A bunch of the Brothers yelling gleefully ran to fasten the net around my prostrate body. Soon I was their helpless prisoner, as though in a cocoon. I tried to strike at them through the few openings but without results.

They simply guffawed at my frustrated efforts, and gave not a hint as to what trick they were playing. "We've got you, Riordan!" I had to admit they did.

Of course I felt mad and swore that I'd remember all who were involved, however, they continued to laugh and make certain I was securely trussed up. I kept lashing out at them when I managed to rearrange the netting, but did little damage. "Now, take it easy and relax," one of them advised. "We're going to take you on a trip you're going to enjoy.

Down the stairs they carried me, and placed my "cocoon" in a convertible with the top down. Some Brothers jumped in and off we drove followed by three other cars. We stopped at the womens' quadrangles. They ceremoniously transported me to one of the Sorority Houses where they dumped me inside the entryway. They discussed going through the inside door but found it locked. One rang the doorbell and they took off wishing me a good-night. Their laughter drove me into a fury until the door opened, revealing a lovely young lady.

"Oh my gosh!" she exclaimed.

I quickly identified myself as to my name, school, Fraternity and explained the probable reason I was there in such a condition. If I were to be the main part of a joke, I wanted it to be a legitimate joke.

"I better get some help," she said.

Soon, I was surrounded by a large group of coeds that steadily increased in size. Most wore robes, and many had hair in curlers or bobbie pins. "Let's get him inside." It took at least a dozen of them to pull me and my net through the inner door.

They stared at me mischievously as though I were a cute trapped animal. Indeed, looking at them, I felt like a trapped animal.

"Are those boxer shorts?" one asked.

"Well ah no," I replied hesitating. "I believe they're called Jockey shorts."

They all giggled. "You must be awfully cold."

"Well, ah as a matter of fact I am. If you'd all sort of press in around me, I'm sure you could warm me up."

111

Many of them did and it was remarkable how quickly I heated up.

"Are you being a naughty boy?" asked a real lovely.

"How could I be? I'm completely trapped in this cargo net."

"Yes, yes that's what we must do," one said. "Get him out of the net."

"No hurry." I observed.

Try as they would, they couldn't free me. "Poor dear," commented another lovely.

"We'll have to cut through the ropes." This proved to be a momentous task. There weren't any substantial knives around, so the going turned out to be very slow. I still felt in no hurry, so I didn't offer to help. They served me hot chocolate, cookies, candy, cake and gummy bears.

Inevitably, Mrs. Hays, an attractive lady who was Housemother, and who I knew slightly, appeared. "I guess you couldn't have done this by yourself."

"No, ma'am."

She hurried along the sawing on the ropes and unfortunately sent the lovelies off to their respective rooms. "I sometimes wonder what we're all coming to."

"Yes, ma'am. If you hand me the knife, I'll work on the ropes. They're pretty thick." After quite a bit of work, I was free.

"Now," sighed Mrs. Hays, "what are we going to do with you?"

"Well, ma'am. I'll just run back up to my House."

She shook her head vigorously. "In your underwear? Of course not, it's after midnight, you might be kicked out of school -- not that you might not deserve it."

Spreading my newly freed hands, I said, "I'm really only a victim, ma'am."

"Come on," she ordered, "you'll stay in my apartment and I'll drive you back in the morning."

Luckily, Mrs. Hays had a large frame. Her fur coat came close to fitting over and covering parts of me. I slept in the coat under a light blanket on her sofa.

Next morning she arranged for me to enjoy a sumptuous breakfast in her living room. Shortly after, she drove me to the north quads still wearing her fur coat over my shorts. I thanked her profusely and promised to return her coat at the earliest possible moment.

As I strode through the parking lot a couple of guys stared at me. "Must have been quite a night," observed the first one.

"I never knew you were into fur, Riordan," said the other.

When I entered my House, the Brothers who hadn't been involved in the mischief wanted to know where I'd been.

"I've spent these last few hours in heaven." I announced pompously. "Let me amend that. I've spent these last few hours <u>close</u> to heaven."

You've probably heard the beautiful song, "The Sweetheart of Sigma Omicron." There were twenty-six national fraternities at Northwestern, but for some reason, our chief rival always seemed to be Sigma Omicron. Perhaps, it was because we both had unusually outstanding groups of men. We vied for top honors against each other in many campus activities.

Sigma Omicron always endeavored to give the impression of being a first class outfit. And, it was. Their house featured a huge front porch with an impressive canopy of tasteful green and white over it. On each side were the Greek letters denoting Sigma Omicron.

Yes, this definitely bespoke of wealth and class; the only fraternity on the entire campus with an awning. I began to bring this fact up, subtly, in many conversations. I'd say something artful and noncommital like, "Just who the hell do they think they are?"

This raised the ire of quite a few not so fortunate as to be able to lounge under a luxurious canopy. I noticed, with some satisfaction, fellows passing the Omi house, and flicking their cigarette butts on the canopy. Most simply rolled off, but those few that remained proved a theory I'd harbored for some time - it would burn - albeit slowly, the damn thing definitely burned.

This was one of the few times I regretted I didn't smoke, nevertheless I knew, as a Phi Delt gentleman, neither I nor any of my Brothers would perform such a dastardly deed. I did enjoy a feeling of elation, however, as others rid themselves of their butts in this manner, particularly at night, when I could observe an ever widening, red-rimmed hole.

The situation got so bad, the Omis stationed a couple of guys on upper floors armed with water buckets. This proved to be too little, too late. Their once proud and glorious canopy looked like Swiss cheese. They finally were forced to tear the tattered remnants down.

We discussed the recent bad fortune of Sigma Omicron at the Phi Delt house. Some sage echoed the feelings of all the Brothers, when he observed, "How terribly unfortunate."

Although our competition could have been classified as "reasonably friendly," toward the end of my Freshman year, I was put in charge of harassing the "Omis." This was a position of considerable prestige, but it demanded action.

My unofficial term of harasser was soon coming to a close. I had to go out in a blaze of glory. The Sigma Omicron Spring Formal loomed up on my calendar, only a week away. That should be the time to strike. But how? I wracked my brain for ideas.

Time grew short. I tossed and turned in my bunk at night, hardly able to sleep. I had to come up with something, a gem. Then as the sun began to brighten the sky on an early May morning, I thought I saw the light. Was this the dawning I had so desperately sought? It would take incredible coordination, but approaching could be my finest hour.

I got all our Pledges together that evening, and a few interested Actives, who could spare the time. I issued them bushel-baskets, and explained. "I want you to comb Evanston, and fill these with doggie excrement."

"You mean dog-shit?" one guy gasped in disbelief.

"That's precisely correct!"

Most of them grumbled, and I couldn't blame their feelings of disgust. I told them I'd be right in there, picking up the stuff. I'd learned in the Army, a good officer never orders his men to do something he won't do himself.

Some still voiced mild objections, and a few began to remember once forgotten duties. Then, I revealed my Master Plan. Enthusiasm quickly ran wild. Our small group spread out around the city, a determined gang of "pooper-scoopers."

We quickly found out that Evanston was a mighty clean city. It sure seemed a tough job to find dog crap, in bulk quantities at any rate.

We added planning to our random search. There were few apartment buildings, however, a large group of us watched these carefully. When wealthy dowagers took "Fido" or "Pierre" out for a walk, we were always close by. There usually was a reward in the end.

So energetic were our efforts, that by Friday night, we had seventeen bags of canine feces hidden on our fourth floor. The stench was awful. Those Brothers who slept up there had to find temporary accommodations downstairs. One, Bob Roberts, who had worked diligently on the collecting, complained, "Gee, I helped collect the crap. I want to zap the Omis as much as anybody, but moving out of my sack to a couch...and everything else...it's too much to ask."

<u>Yeh</u>, I thought, as I continued to plan the strategy and logistics of the operation, <u>the troops are never happy unless they're griping.</u> We'd need twenty good men plus an efficient Commander tomorrow night. I hoped I wouldn't blow it. I'd of course, be the Commander.

Saturday night, or to be perfectly accurate Sunday morning, most of the members of our Chapter were somewhere close to the Omi house by 1:45 a.m. Included were twenty intrepid, face-blackened commandos with their inspiring leader. The sorority girls had to be signed in by 2:00 a.m., so we wouldn't have long to wait.

The Sigma Omicrons could be counted on to drive directly back to their house. Evanston, the national headquarters of the Woman's Christian Temperance Union, lacked any entertainment at 2 o'clock in the morning. We were grateful for that fact.

Sure enough, about 2:10, they began to arrive, looking sharp in their white dinner jackets. Now, I'm certain the Omis didn't drink any more than we did, but this had been a festive occasion and many of them were pretty well oiled. Sure, I had been counting on this. By 2:25, according to our head-count, almost all of them were there.

Following their great tradition, they formed a large semi-circle in their huge living room, and linked arm in arm, began to sing "The Sweetheart of Sigma Omicron. "It was beautiful!

It inspired us to spring into action. We gingerly placed seventeen double-thick paper bags full of dog-shit at appropriate intervals on their front porch, and quickly doused them with lighter fluid.

Now, the Omis, who we could easily see through the French windows, were singing, "Not Every Man Can Wear the Blue Cross," a fine tribute to their attractive pin. It sure was impressive. Before any tears trickled down our cheeks, we lit each bag.

Flames gushed upward as we dashed for cover, taking positions from where we could observe. Some spots got pretty crowded.

Nothing happened for a couple of minutes. These felt much longer than 120 seconds to us. The Omis continued singing, verse after verse. Our seventeen flaring torches lighted the campus. At last shouts of "Fire! Fire!" came from inside.

The white-jacketed bunch poured onto the porch, paused to assess the situation, and then began stomping on the fiery bags. Quickly their entire chapter answered the call to duty.

Sigma Omicron patent leather shoes pushed through pounds of dog-shit. Carefully pressed formal trousers were mired to their knees in the stinking excrement. Feces from a myriad of breeds liberally spattered crisp white dinner jackets.

The slop must have been slippery. Even after the flames had died down, many Omis were sliding and belly-flopping on the porch. Suddenly, one of them yelled out, "Hey, this is dog-shit."

Our guys were laughing so hard, they could hardly make it back home. We double locked the front door, posted sentries, and climbed in triumph to the top-floor of our house, where a quarter-barrel had been hidden. This was strictly forbidden by University rules, but we had a lot to celebrate.

Everybody compared notes as to the details of what he had witnessed. A once hesitant Bob Roberts, hardly able to talk through his glee blurted out, "and then old Gordie tripped and slid face first in the crap." We dissolved in hilarity, many of us falling on the floor with laughter. "I'll never forget the looks on their faces."

"Well," I said, holding a full glass, and a bottle of champagne that had been specially purchased as a gesture of confidence in me, "here's to the Omis. They always did have a special <u>air</u> about them!"

"TAKE IT RAT!"

Millie and Jane were in the kitchen after removing the last dishes from the table. The dinner had been only fair, but we really weren't too interested in our food.

Here Bill and I were in the modest house rented by two waitresses - not Northwestern coeds - and our imaginations of what the next couple of hours might bring were lurid almost beyond belief. "Can we help with the dishes?" I called out.

"No, no thanks," answered Millie, "we'll just stack 'em, and then see what develops."

Bill winked at me and I winked back. I honestly felt a little guilty being without my buddy Norris Fester. But, when I explained to him, he had understood.

"Yeh, well I suppose you couldn't cut Bill out when he was right there in the restaurant."

"That's true, Norris, Bill was sitting right beside me when I made the date."

"Yeh, well that's O.K. What did you say their names were?"

I wanted to above board with my friend. "Millie and Jane. Millie's much better looking. They've got a small house behind that big Victorian place on Grange Avenue."

"Sounds like you two are in like tall burglars," observed Fester. "You can bet we'll all be waiting up to hear the gory details."

I figured the "gory details" were about to commence when the girls returned with four small glasses and a bottle. "Would you guys like some Creme-de-Menthe?"

"Sure."

"Thank you very much," I said getting up to help.

Although neither Bill nor I smoked, we all had cigarettes with our liqueur. It took about an hour of mundane chit-chat to drain the bottle. When it was finally empty, Jane got off the sofa and announced. "I'm going to show Bill the rest of the house." Bill giggled and grabbed her hand. When they were almost out of the room, Jane turned and said, "Don't wait up for us."

"I'm glad they like each other," said Millie, "aren't you?"

"Oh yes," I replied, "I'm really glad."

"Do you think we could like each other, too?" asked Millie.

"Sure, I'll bet we could like each other a lot."

"Well, why don't you come over and sit real close beside me?" Millie sat in an overstuffed chair that was designed for only one.

I got up and tried to sit next to her. She moved over as far as she could and finally got up. "Why don't you sit on the chair and I'll sit on your lap?" she asked.

"That sounds great to me," I replied.

In less than a second she was on my lap. Her perfume seemed the sexiest cheap stuff I'd ever smelled. We embraced, rather casually at first, then more deeply. She blew in my ear, and whispered in it, "Do you mind if I ask you a rather personal question?"

"A personal question?" I echoed. We kissed, again. She bit my lip. "Why of course not."

She touched her nose to mine. "Do you ever get W.H.T.?"

"Ah W.H.T.? What's W.H.T.?

She pulled me closer. "Some people call it 'wandering hand trouble!"

Her hair cascaded over me. The curves of her Jasmine scented body were like sensual magnets. They inexorably attracted my spasmatically clutching hands. I blurted, "I'll bet I could develop a case of chronic W.H.T."

She gave a sexy laugh and licked her lips. I had read enough to know what was coming. I felt about to burst.

Suddenly a bright light swept the room. An explosion shook the furniture causing a vase to topple and break. This is sex, I thought, raw, passionate, unadulterated sex.

Millie jumped up and ran to the open front window. Had I gone too far? "What the hell's all that noise?" she yelled. I moved with a bit of difficulty and joined her, looking out. Their house faced an alley which was brightly lighted by the headlights of two cars standing next to each other. A body lay about thirty feet in front of the cars and two guys whose hands were tied cowered next to the inert form.

One guy yelled toward the car, "Please Guido, please, we didn't rat on you." I could smell the cordite fumes that accounted for the body laying in the alley. "Please," continued the pleading voice, "Guido, you got the wrong guys. We didn't squeal on you. Don't blast us."

Jane and Bill appeared and joined us at the window. "What was that explosion?" asked Jane.

"Yeh, what's going on?"

A tall man wearing a dark coat and gray Homburg strode from near the cars and slapped the two trussed offenders across their faces. Then, he walked back into the darkness near the automobiles.

"It's a mob killing," said Millie, "right in front of our house. They've killed one, and now they're going to shoot the other two."

"They're begging for their lives," said Jane, wide-eyed.

"Please Guido, don't blast us," one began to sob, "you've got the wrong guys."

A voice answered vehemently from near the darkness. "Nobody's bigger than the Syndicate. You guys are getting what you deserve." Somehow, the voice sounded vaguely familiar.

Suddenly, the intended victims turned and sprinted down the alley, still bathed in the glow of the headlights. A shotgun belched flame once, then again. One squealer's body catapulted in the air, the second was cut down in a burst of sub-machine gun fire.

"Get down on the floor," yelled Millie. "They might come after us."

While the four of us lay on the floor, the vaguely familiar voice shouted, "That's what happens to squealers. Nobody bucks the Syndicate."

Bill whispered one word, "Fester."

"Yeh," I acknowledged soto voce, "Fester, the rat."

"What did you say?" asked Millie.

"Nothing," I answered. "I was sort of praying or something."

We heard the roar of powerful engines and tortured rubber as the "Syndicate" cars took off like scalded cats.

Jane began blubbering uncontrollably, "They killed them. Murdered them in cold blood. Right in front of us...in cold blood... ...right in front..." her ravings were drowned out by the wail of Evanston Police sirens.

There were plenty of excited witnesses besides us. Eager citizens from two nearby apartment buildings repeated exactly what we had seen, and even established where each victim had dropped under a hail of lead. Two facts mystified the Police, who took names, and were very thorough. They couldn't find any trace of blood, nor could they locate any of the bodies.

As soon as we were free to go, Millie said, "Well, maybe we'll see you guys, again."

"Oh, yeh, sure," I said.

Jane, still crying, referred to us as "bad luck."

When we got back to our Fraternity House, although lights were on in all the rooms, it seemed eerily quiet. No one occupied the living room, and the halls were empty. Not even a radio played.

We climbed the stairs to the third floor and stopped in front of my room. Absolute silence. I tried my door. It was unlocked. I opened it slowly.

Norris sat behind my desk wearing a black cashmere overcoat with a velvet collar and a gray Homburg. he smoked a thick cigar. On my desk lay a Thompson sub-machine gun.

"Oh, you studs back already?" He blew smoke toward my face. "How did you guys make out?"

"Like tall burglars, Guido!" I yelled.

Then I grabbed the sub-machine gun off the desk and while he laughed so hard, he lost his Homburg, I fired the rest of the blank bullets at his gleefully squirming body.

THE UNKNOWN ADMIRER

Stealing hardly ever seemed to be a problem on the "men's end" of the Northwestern campus. Most of the dorms and houses were arranged roughly in quadrangles on the university's northernmost part.

The door to the Phi Delt house was always unlocked as were those of the other fraternities. While we had keys to our rooms, nobody ever locked his door. We, of course, trusted each other.

One afternoon I returned from class to see some guy I'd never seen before, going through my dresser drawers.

"Hello," I said, "I'm Lee Riordan. Can I help you?"

He smiled, waved aside my introduction and carefully returned my favorite orange and green shirt to its proper place in my drawer.

In the doorway he paused long enough to say, "You do have exquisite taste."

Then he quickly left. I never saw him, again.

But, I knew he was an excellent judge of sartorial splendor.

A STRONG BODY AND A WEAK MIND

Most universities would eagerly recruit a guy, any guy, though he had barely graduated from some high-school, if he was a football star, and could run forty yards in 4.6 seconds with an anvil tucked under each arm.

Most universities were not Northwestern, however, where other additional standards had to be met. A prospect must have graduated in the upper third of his secondary school class, and displayed proficiency in a battery of entrance exams. Our beloved University believed in the highest academic standards for all its students, including its football players. I'm still proud of that fact.

But, I do remember an occasional exception. One of these rarities, was Bronko Granite. The coaches elevated him from the Freshman squad to the Varsity after an unusual incident.

We wore a conglomeration of old, faded, beat up jerseys to practice. One afternoon, Bronko had been issued one with a lot of holes in it. When our seven assistant coaches came on the field, they spied him, and one shouted, "Hey Bronk, where'd you get that jersey? You look like a Swiss cheese."

They stopped laughing when he ran over, fists clenched, a wild expression on his face, and screamed, "Who say dat--who say dat to Bronko?"

A defensive coach, sporting a nervous smile quickly said, "Look Bronko, you been doin' great...from now on we want you running with the Varsity." He probably was afraid Bronko would take them <u>all</u> on. I think he would have.

The other guys sort of resented Bronko. I did too, but I also kind of felt sorry for him. He never seemed to talk with anybody. One Sunday afternoon, before our grueling schedule of games had begun, a bunch of us were horsing around with a basketball on one of the outdoor courts. Bronko came walking by, all bundled up, even though it was in the 80's. "Hey Bronko," I said moving toward him, "how about shooting some baskets?"

"God damn sissy sport," he gritted through clenched teeth, without slowing his pace at all.

To begin the season, we played Navy at Philadelphia, before a packed stadium. After we ran up quite a lead, they put Bronko in, on defense, of course. It really takes more brains to play offense. I spent most of my time on defense too.

No, I wasn't in the lineup when he came on the playing field, but I thought I could read the lips of our defensive Captain--"See man in blue jersey and gold helmet carrying the ball. You kill Bronko--Bronko kill!" Granite's head bobbed up and down as he moved to linebacker, my usual position.

The Navy fullback got a pitch-out on a misdirection play. Bronko didn't go for the fake, he just stood there riveted, trying to decide what to do. A Navy blocker bounced off him. You could tell the instant he saw the ball. He jumped like a scalded bull, but he didn't tackle the approaching fullback; he "atomized" him. he ran through the space where Mr. Navy had been, and KABOOM, neither of them was there

135

anymore. Bronko appeared about twenty yards down the field, as he flopped on the still bouncing ball. It took the Middies awhile to reassemble their fullback and place all the parts on a stretcher.

Some of the highly partisan Navy fans began to boo, unjustifiably, I thought. Any student of physics would have recognized it had been a classic case of a mere mortal being run over by a locomotive.

Suddenly, Bronko rushed the nearer stands. he must have decided the cat-calls were unfair, too, and wanted to "punish' the 50,000 people on that side of the field. He apparently did a good job because, while his white jersey disappeared into the melee, quite a number of bodies flew out of the pile, half of them police.

By the time we arrived, he'd decided they'd had enough. The game officials didn't know what to do. They couldn't come up with a penalty that covered a participant attacking spectators, but we kept Bronko out of the other stands, anyway.

About four weeks later, back in Evanston, we celebrated the

completion of something new in our practice area. Three football fields were available to us, Dyche Stadium, and two others close by. Now, one of these had been entirely closed in by an eight-foot fence of 2 X 4s. "This is our new 'band-box' men," announced our head coach, "we'll hold our secret practices in here."

For some reason, the walls of our band-box had been painted the color of rotting limes. Even Bronko felt irritated by the awful hue. "Damned baby shit green," he growled.

One afternoon, we were loosening up in the band-box before the coaching staff came on the field, when a few guys decided to "needle" Bronko. "Hey Granite, do you think you could punch a hole in that fence?"

"Hell yeah, Bronko knock da whole damn ting down."

We stood around to watch, expecting him to go up and smash it with one of his beefy fists. Instead, he got into a linebacker stance about five yards away, then charged the green wall, head first. There was a loud splintering crash.

A gaping, jagged hole appeared as Bronko's wide body burst through to the opposite side.

He had demolished a good eight feet of fence. We cheered and clapped. Bronko trotted back, acknowledging our plaudits with a gleeful look in his eyes. I'd never seen him happy before. He stopped in front of a solid piece of fencing, crouched in his stance, and drove forward again with the same result. "Give him another half-hour and he'll have the whole thing knocked down." We laughed, but we were impressed.

Our coaches weren't. They were just plain mad, and let Bronko and his audience know it. We'd have to repair the fence before practice the next Monday. It looked like it would be quite a job. Bronko simply grinned foolishly, oblivious to the green paint smeared over the top of his helmet.

A couple days later, he missed a home game. We won easily. Later, someone said he'd seen Bronko's mid-quarter grade report and it was all "F's." When asked, one of the coaches dismissed it lightly, "Granite? Oh yeah, he's gone."

The following Monday our repair crew came on the field an hour early, wearing the usual light Monday attire of sweat-suits and helmets. We were expected, because next to the band-box was a pile of 2 X 4's, saws, hammers, nails, two buckets of green paint and some other carpentry equipment. I measured some wood, laid it on two horses and began sawing. Some guys merely stood and watched. "Well come on, you stiffs," I yelled, "we're all in this together."

"Hey Riordan, you think you could do what he did?"

I stopped cutting. "What 'ya mean?"

The challenge seemed to come from the entire bunch. "We mean, could you punch a hole--like Bronko did?"

"Hell yes," I replied, "but I'm not that stupid."

"Bet you couldn't," someone goaded. "Let's see ya do it before the coaches get here."

I knew the coaches wouldn't be on the field for at least an hour. We were expected to have the fence fixed by then. But as a "starter," I couldn't lose face. "Listen, I'll take you slobs on."

"No, the fence."

"I'll take any two of you slobs."

They knew they had me, "No, the fence Riordan."

I dropped my saw, dashed onto the playing surface, and with hardly a pause drove fast and powerfully for the green barrier.

When I woke up my helmet was off, and trainers were kneeling over me, one putting an iced cloth on my forehead, and the other wafting ammonia fumes into my nostrils. "What happened to you?"

My body screeched with pain and my neck felt like its gears were stripped. "N..n..nothing," I gasped.

"You must have thrown a bad block," one of them speculated.

"You sure you're O.K.?" the other asked.

Somehow I forced myself to a sitting position. "Yeh, sure, I'm O.K."

The trainers closed up their cases and left, just as the coaches came on the field. One approached me at a trot. he was only a blur as I groped for my helmet and tried to focus my eyes. "What the hell

Riordan, get off your ass."
Painfully, I got to my feet.
Angrily, he looked me up and down.
"How come you got Granite's
helmet?"

Yes, I could just make out the
green paint on the top of my
helmet, like Bronko's. I mumbled
something.

"Well, we won't miss him," he
said, spitting in the grass, "he
sure was a dumb bastard."

"Yessir--right," I agreed,
wobbling toward the lines of guys
straining at calisthenics. "_I_ sure
as hell won't miss him."

There weren't any "snap-courses" at Northwestern. In all my four years, I never found any. Sure, some were harder than others, but even I needed to study for Music Appreciation. Yet, I thoroughly enjoyed it.

I began my major in Engineering, so I had quite a few tough subjects. I transferred to the Communications School, not because I couldn't do the work, but because I had found new interests.

It may sound cornball, but I really wanted to learn as much as I could. If the course wouldn't interfere with football, and the content interested me; no matter how difficult its reputation, I'd sign up.

Right from the first day, "Comparative Anatomy" looked pretty ominous, The students were practically all male pre-meds carrying briefcases. Even the only two girls in the class carried them. Standing stiffly like SS men, along the walls of the slanted lecture hall, were the teaching and

142

lab assistants, who were rumored to have flunked out of Medical School. They knew the Pre-Meds needed at least a "B" in the course, though by the surly expressions on their faces, I could see they'd make certain no one in this class would ever get to Medical School.

Finally, our Professor arrived. I dubbed him, "Doctor Chill Factor" even before he spoke. He looked like an executioner.

A master of intimidation, he rambled on about how tough this course was, how we could expect a test on any of our three lecture days, and how difficult and critical our three hour lab session on Thursdays would be. He also proudly stated that no one had ever gotten an "A" while he'd been running things; about 7% received "B's," approximately 33% "C's," and the remaining 60% "D's" and "F's."

Everyone sagged perceptibly at this last announcement. Then, he really shocked us. "For our next class session, I want each of you to hand in a detailed, complete history of your sex-life." After our initial surprise, all eyes turned to the two girls, who blushed and fidgeted nervously. I raised my hand.

He seemed to ignore me, but eventually he said, "Yes."

I stood up. "Will a three by five card do?"

The class roared with laughter.

Dr. Chill Factor fixed me with a beady stare. "What is your name, young man?" No doubt he thought I'd make a fine specimen for the lab.

I told him my name adding, "I can turn in my card after class, today."

Everyone guffawed, almost out of their seats. Even one teaching assistant came close to cracking a smile.

It was the last time anyone in that class laughed out loud until the end of the quarter.

Over the years I attended Northwestern, I had many "pledge sons," younger fellows I sort of looked after as they became acclimated to school and the Fraternity. These "sons" were assigned under an excellent system that helped newer guys have the benefit of an older member's experience.

Bud was one of my most memorable sons because he never failed to be full of surprises. A real likeable chap, he let me know right from the start he was short of money. "I never thought this place was going to be so expensive. Where can I get a board-job?"

I asked around, but board-jobs were prize possessions in both Fraternity and Sorority Houses, and they went early. I found him one at the YMCA, but he didn't like the idea of it for some reason. "I'll just skip dinner. I can get along on two meals."

I explained how the Fraternity was very flexible in its payment plans, and offered to speak to the

145

house manager on his behalf, but he said "No." So, I sneaked him a sandwich from the kitchen most every evening. Around 10:30 another fellow from a different fraternity also named "Bud" came around selling sandwiches. My Bud would buy one. Sometimes I'd buy two and give him one, and money often was a problem for me. Well, I figured it was for a good cause.

"What am I going to do for clothes?" he blurted out one day. "You've got some great clothes, Lee."

He was right there. Now and then I'd be called to work as a model in a fashion show, and often got to keep some of the clothing. My wardrobe would be classified as excellent. "Just help yourself," I told him.

And, he did. While my stuff was big on him I sometimes thought it was a special style show featuring me, walking down the stairs. How he loved my sky blue cashmere sport coat. It spent most of the time in his closet, or on his back.

"Our razor is broken," he announced one morning, holding the almost new appliance. I hunted up a

146

blade and cut myself a few times. I felt irritated by things besides the shave.

"Hey Lee, my folks are coming in for Homecoming."

"Why that's great, Bud. I'll really look forward to meeting them," I said sincerely.

"Well, I want them to meet you too. I've written to them how you've helped me." He paused with excitement. "They're coming for two reasons because Homecoming Day is my birthday."

"Gee, congratulations!"

I bought Bud a small lapel device that identified our Fraternity.

His folks were grand. Homecoming night I saw what they bought him. "Wait 'til you see it, Lee."

"Sure, where is it?"

"Outside!"

"Outside?"

"Sure, come on!" he grabbed my arm.

In the Phi Delt parking lot stood a red Cadillac convertible. "Isn't it a beaut?"

I surveyed it for a couple of minutes, then intoned. "Let's say it correctly, Bud, with careful and accurate articulation. Isn't <u>our</u> Cadillac, beautiful?!!"

Returning to the campus one fall, I found our fraternity house had acquired an unexpected guest. It was a large box turtle. One of the Brothers had brought it back from Army Reserve Camp. We named the turtle Oscar.

For some reason, Oscar seemed to feel special affection for me. Perhaps, he recognized that I really liked turtles. I'd pick him up and talk to him. Maybe he sensed I'd once had twenty-six swamp turtles, when I was a kid.

The guys treated him like a pet dog, fed him, sat him on their knees, and generally let him enjoy the run of the house. He could even climb the stairs because he was big enough to reach from one riser to the next. Oh, it was very slow going, but nothing stopped Oscar when he was determined.

One day, he "clumped" into my third floor room. He stretched his neck and stared at me with those penetrating hazel eyes, and hissed, like a snake. When I reached to pick him up, he drew in his handsome head and retracted his limbs. I sat back, waiting for Oscar to make the next move. he continued to eye me, from the protection of his magnificent shell. Finally, he eased into a corner and went to sleep.

While he regularly traveled throughout the house, he'd found a home in my room. I got a wooden box where he could retire quietly, or even nap in his leisure moments, and kept a dish of water close by. He lounged often in a corner, which I'm certain he considered "his corner." When some of the fellows were looking for him, they'd often say, "He must be in Riordan's room." And, there they usually found him. Many guys fed him when he roamed -- he liked hamburger -- but, I think I was the only one to hold regular conversations with him. He also loved music, Bach especially.

The supposedly more learned scholars pointed out that he couldn't possibly hear, only feel vibrations from the music. But, I knew, Oscar liked Bach's vibrations best.

One evening after dinner, some of us relaxed in our huge living room, watching Oscar slowly travel across the thick carpeting. Directly in the middle of the room, where he could be seen by all, he paused, dropping an oblong white egg, then moved a few inches and dropped another.

"What's wrong with Oscar?" somebody yelled.

Someone more astute shouted, "Ye Gods, Oscar's a woman."

The entire multitude gradually stood as this reality of life engulfed it. Oscar hissed proudly. "He's an Oscarina!"

The Brothers expressed many feelings of awe and confusion. "Maybe male turtles lay eggs."

"I would have sworn she was a virgin, like all Northwestern girls."

"You sly bastard Riordan -- keeping a woman in your room."

"Yeh, geez, that's really disgusting."

A couple of biology students retrieved the eggs, assuring everyone they would take special care of them.

I picked up Oscar -- or Oscarina and started to go upstairs, accompanied by a few catcalls.

"The University has rules against what you're doing."

"Lecher."

"Riordan, you filthy make-out artist!"

The next evening, most of the chapter attended a "What to do about Oscarina" meeting. It was run by Biology and Medical students.

One of them asked, "Ah Riordan, where is he -- that is, where is she?"

"She's upstairs listening to Bach."

"Now, look, she can't possibly 'hear' the music."

"Well, why don't you go up and tell her that?" I responded. "Or maybe you should write her a note."

After they assured us the eggs were safe, they delivered a short lecture on reproduction in the turtle. Oscarina was indeed a virgin and had not been defiled by the rampant libido of a reprehensible member of her species. The eggs were obviously in good shape, but must be fertilized as quickly as possible. They described the process in considerable detail.

"But, where can we find a male box turtle?"

"Yeh, not much chance in Evanston, Illinois."

"We do have a predicament," said one of the Med students, sternly. He got to his feet. "Our only hope is a surrogate. He must, of course, be a volunteer."

Everyone seemed to be impressed with the gravity of the problem. Gradually, one by one, they looked in my direction. I had no trouble reading their minds. I jumped up and walked rapidly to the door.

Our resident medical authority called after me, "It would be an act of extreme valor, Lee -- extreme valor!"

Applause had just begun as I made a quick exit.

Shortly afterward, the medico-biology team came to our room, deposited both eggs in Oscarina's box and bade us a fervent "good luck" before closing our door respectfully. The turtle seemed to grin happily. I sighed, certainly not with resignation, but anyhow turned off Bach's "Air On A G String."

For the next couple of days, not much happened. Oh, I complained about the "Do Not Disturb" sign some wag kept hanging on my door. Brothers questioned -- "How are things going with the family?" and "Have you two talked turtle as yet?" But, actually things were pretty close to normal.

On the fourth day after the discovery, when I returned from some classes. I spied a banner strung tautly across our porch. it proclaimed, "Congratulations Lee."

A bunch of guys, giggling like idiots, followed me to the third floor room. Oscarina sat in her box, craning her neck joyously, along with two baby box turtles.

Champagne corks popped. It seemed most of our group had suddenly materialized, shouting and laughing. A full glass of champagne and an open box of cigars were thrust in my hands. While one of the gleeful crowd lighted my stogie, yelling "Congratulations," repeatedly, I tried to protest.

"Look, I swear, I never got near those eggs -- not even close."

They all guffawed and began singing "For He's a Jolly Good Fellow."

Soon, out came the cameras. Oscarina squatted on the desk; I in a chair behind her holding the little ones. Flashbulbs popped while arguments blazed as to which baby looked more like me. "There's a terrific resemblance in profile. It's really startling." Oscarina hissed. So did the babies.

Around my neck hung a huge sign announcing one of the many nicknames I picked up at Northwestern. In eight-inch letters it simply said, "Daddy Lee."

My English professor walked up the aisle slowly, returning the initial test papers for this class in Russian Literature. I gasped when he handed me mine with a "C" minus on it. Next to the grade written in red were the words, "Please See Me."

Apparently, most of my classmates had done considerably better, judging from their grins and exchanges of mutual satisfaction. In my immediate area I could see four "A's" and two "B" plusses on display.

Professor Kutchitoff returned to the front of the room and said, "Most of you did quite well. I see you're happy with your grades." There was a general mumble of assent.

"Is there anyone unhappy with his grade?"

Might make a good impression to be honest. I raised my hand.

"Oh, yes, Mr. Riordan, I too am disappointed in your grade, especially with your Russian heritage."

My classmates appeared mildly amused at finding a dummy in class.

"May I ask," the Professor continued, "how you did in high school?"

I couldn't resist, "You mean in Russian Literature?"

The class laughed loudly.

"No," he answered without any reaction to my "gag." "I mean in high school generally."

I thought carefully before I spoke. I knew Northwestern's reputation for scholastics, and I was a good student who would now speak for football players, Russian backgrounds and war veterans. I proudly replied, "I was Salutatorian in a graduating class of 467!"

"That's very impressive, Mr. Riordan," said Professor Kutchitoff, "perhaps you'll allow me a small bit of research."

He then surveyed the members of our entire class about their high school records.

Everyone else had been a Valedictorian.

One of the guys who worked a "board-job" with me was a good looking transfer student named Jethro. While he studied hard, and did his share in the kitchen, he seemed to take life real easy, and always maintained an even temper. Like a couple of other fellows in our house, he'd served in submarines, and they too were easygoing and sociable.

When we weren't pushing food, or washing dishes, we board-jobbers talked a lot about athletics, girls, our fraternity brothers, the war, and our ambitions for the future.

Jethro said most guys in "subs" were pretty coolheaded because they lived for lengthy periods in confined quarters where small incidents of friction could cause big problems. Before being accepted for underwater duty, everyone had to pass a battery of psychological tests to prove he had a calm, hard to ruffle disposition.

"Yeh, you get a lot of time to do plenty of objective thinking and planning on a submarine. Sure, I've got emotions," he admitted, "but I'm realistic about the future and why I came here to Northwestern."

I'd sort of wondered why he'd transferred from a school in Indiana to N.U., and I told him so.

"Well, I did a lot of that objective thinking before I decided to come here. I analyzed the situation. Let's face it, any girl who's going to Northwestern has to be loaded, right?"

"Gee," I said somewhat thoughtfully, "the costs are awfully high. I suppose you're right."

"Sure, there are 'poor' guys on scholarships, the G.I. Bill, and other deals, but there aren't any 'poor' girls. You know what I mean. I've seen you making time with Daphne."

"Daphne?" I repeated, "Oh, yeh Daphne--we're only friends."

"Of course, you know her old man's Board Chairman of General Electronics!"

"He is? Heck, I didn't know that. How'd you find out?"

"Listen Lee, you've got to keep up with that sort of information.

Why half the girls here have Dads who're rated in Dun and Bradstreet."

"Sure I suppose you're right. I simply never thought about it."

"Well, you better start. That's the big reason I came here. I'm going to get me a rich wife--and I don't mean just wealthy--I mean _filthy_ rich, so I'll never have to work again."

I watched Jethro play up to a number of girls whose backgrounds and financial standings I assumed he'd checked out. Shortly before his graduation, he latched on to one in particular. She was extremely attractive and personable, but I felt certain he knew the _really_ _important_ things about her.

Dallas is an attractive city. I've only visited it six times since college, but while there I always look up Jethro. I can count on him to show me a fine time. He picks me up in the newest red Jaguar, then it's tennis at "The Club," followed by an extended luncheon poolside with pleasant light conversation. Later, after superb food and drink at his "Hacienda," we sip our after dinner libations while floating in the pool among fragrant gardenias and water blossoms.

When we part, he never fails to endear himself to me by making the same distressful observation, "I guess you missed it Old Buddy. You just didn't learn anything in school. The last work I ever did was that god-damned board-job."

TABLE MANNERS

On Sunday nights, dinner was never served at the House. We had to fend for ourselves, and when a group of us had some extra money, accompanied by voracious appetites we'd get one of the Brothers to drive to a fine Chicago restaurant.

This evening we ran into fellow students waiting to be seated, among them McLean Stevenson, who we fondly called Mac. He was quite a cut-up on campus. Now, he was off campus.

The Maitre d' was occupied elsewhere, so Stevenson charged ahead yelling, "Come on, I'll find us all a table."

We followed right behind. The place was really crowded, the tables near together, but we kept close to quick-witted Mac. "Hey, there's a couple," he shouted and changed his direction abruptly. He plowed into a gentleman peacefully eating his dinner, and pitched him out of his chair.

When they both regained their feet, Stevenson growled at him, "Dammit mister, why don't you look where you're <u>sitting</u>?"

When I arrived in Evanston to study, sharpen my social graces and play football, I had no idea I would have a part in the demise of a well-known restaurant.

No Sunday evening meal was served anywhere on campus, so everyone had to find somewhere else to eat. Many students grabbed a hamburger or a couple of hot dogs, while a smaller number, those with money, went to some posh place for a full-course dinner.

My G.I. check must have just come through, because this particular Sunday I joined my fraternity brothers Norris Fester, Buzzy Burton, and a guy named Dan when they drove off to find a suitable establishment noted for good food. There were many in the vicinity. We finally decided on one close to a main highway called "The Glowing Embers"

It was crowded, so we stood in line waiting behind a bunch of gold mounted, red-velvet ropes. I could see the appointments were luxurious. The main room was heavily draped and decorated in varying shades of blue. Large booths were built in along all the walls, with attractive tables filling in the mid-section. Where the blue folds cascading from the ceiling came together, exactly in the center of the room, there hung a huge crystal chandelier.

We were trying to determine, among ourselves, why the place was named "The Glowing Embers." None were in evidence. Perhaps, we conjectured, the name might have more appeal to its upper-class family clientele. Just then, the Maitre d' approached and informed us sourly that we could not be seated without ties. We were dressed in jackets and neat sports shirts. We looked clean and sharp.

Fester and Burton protested vehemently, but to no avail. The snobbish bum merely appeared bored and moved on to the next group, pointedly ignoring us. We left.

"We'll ruin this God-damn place," declared Fester when we were outside.

"Damn right," agreed Burton. They'll have to tear the dump down when we get through with it."

We ate somewhere else. I was awfully hungry and so mainly interested in my food. All Norris and Buzzy could do however, was talk about how they were going to "get" the Embers.

I had been a bit miffed, but it didn't bother me that much. A lot of places enforced a "ties only" requirement, and at the time, I accepted it. I sort of forgot about it.

This was not the case with Fester and Burton. They felt we'd been insulted, and vowed revenge.

About a week and a half later, Norris and Buzzy strode into my room. "Sunday night we're all going back to The Glowing Embers," Norris announced, while Buzzy nodded. "I made our reservations, so I'll pick up the check."

The idea of a free dinner certainly appealed to me. "Gee, that's awfully nice of you, Norris. We better remember to wear our ties."

Burton nodded again and said sarcastically, "Don't worry, we will."

Sunday, we arrived at the restaurant just before seven.

Fester slipped a five-dollar bill in the Maitre d's eager fingers and we were quickly ushered to a large table, right under the brightly lighted chandelier.

"Hey, this is very nice," I observed. "All we have to do is wear ties and we become the center of attraction."

"No," answered Norris, speaking to us in a confidential tone. "I asked for this table specifically." Then he said quite loudly, "Yeh, I've had friends tell me the same thing. This place has really gone down hill. A lot of them got sick after eating here."

I didn't know what he was talking about, but because of our location and the volume of his voice many of the other patrons heard him.

"That's right," boomed Buzzy, "they all got sick on their food."

We ordered, and the appetizers, soups and salads slowly arrived. Burton and Fester continued loudly to berate the restaurant, giving more colorful descriptions of how deathly ill many of their personal friends had become after, or even while dining there.

Gradually, most of the other conversations died down. The customers were more or less forced to listen to the vociferous comments emanating from our table. Many of them began to look somewhat disturbed, and a few a little sick. We were the focus of attention.

The Maitre d' came over to Norris and quietly asked if he could tone down the conversation. "What's the matter, didn't I give you enough money?" Fester bellowed at him. His words were like heavy blows, striking throughout the room. "You just don't want people to know the kind of rotten food you've been serving here!" The Maitre d' beat a hasty retreat as our entrees arrived. Perhaps, he thought the generous portions would quiet things down.

I still didn't know what was going on. I felt famished and so did Dan. We both plunged into our savory smelling dinners. Norris and Buzzy began to eat, then started to pick tentatively at their food. All eyes were on them.

"Geez, this is terrible," said Fester, so the entire multitude could hear him.

"Yeh," agreed Burton in a similar voice, "my meat's rotten and the rest is spoiled."

"This fish tastes like it came out of a sewer, it's rancid."

I thought the food was great and stopped wolfing it only to watch our two culprits, who were now somewhat bent over, apparently from stomach cramps. I watched as each one of them surreptitously reached inside his jacket and unscrewed something. Both straightened up and I could barely see the top of a rubber hot water-bottle emerge from their coats.

"Man, my guts are killing me," shouted Burton.

"Oh shit, I'm going to be sick," yelled Fester. With that he made dry retching sounds, convulsed over the table, and squeezed the open hot water-bottle under his jacket. What looked like cold stew belched forth, all over everything.

"I've got to puke too," screamed Burton, ending with a gurgle as he bent over. Stew shot onto our table, collected in pools and dripped off the sides.

They alternated in this retching act of theirs. It mounted in intensity. The dumbfounded restaurant staff simply stood in open mouthed disbelief. I must admit it was disgusting, and tremendously realistic. A voice wailed, "Oh no." A kid started crying. At least two people in separate booths vomited.

Slop, including peas, carrots, and pieces of meat -- whatever had been in the stew -- covered our clothes, our table, and continued dribbling onto the floor.

Norris began picking up individual peas and bits of carrot and ceremoniously munching them. "At least now I've got something decent to eat," he declared in a loud voice.

This was the final straw for many of the diners. Of course, none of them had seen the containers hidden in our heroes' jackets. Quite a number got up to leave. Some were sobbing. A few more got sick.

Burton yelled, "This place has rotten food. It stinks." We made a rapid escape and quickly drove away. People were really streaming out of the place.

When they realized we had gone a safe distance Norris and Buzzy dissolved in a paroxysm of laughter. "We really socked it to them."

"They'll never recover from this," gasped Burton.

"Don't worry," said Fester, "I'll take care of the cleaning bills." His hot water-bottle fell limply to the floor of the car. They both went crazy laughing again.

I felt too stunned to react to anything.

One night, about two weeks later, Norris burst into my room and gleefully yelled, "It's burning! I just heard it on the radio, the damn place is burning!"

"What place?" I asked, rather mystified.

"Why the damn Embers. Come on let's go."

We all piled into his car and roared off toward the restaurant. Ahead, the sky had a red tinge.

It was a real conflagration. Apparently the fire had gotten a big start before the firemen had even arrived. Although they did their best, in a short time nothing remained but crimson-hot steel supports.

"Does it look like it was set?" Buzzy asked one of the firemen holding a hose.

"Yeh," he replied, "it's always closed Monday night and stunk like kerosene."

Over near the car, Fester and Burton exulted. "We did it! Business got so bad they had to burn it down."

"Geez, even the metal is glowing."

"Hey, the whole damn thing's a pile of glowing embers."

They were right, the restaurant had finally earned its name. Norris and Buzzy jumped up and down, joyously repeating, "We did it, we did it. We made the bastards burn it down!"

The story swept through our fraternity almost as fast as the fire had through the unfortunate supper club.

Like it or not all four of us were celebrities. Fester and Burton repeated the details often, constantly bolstering our newly acquired notoriety.

During my four years at Northwestern I had a number of nicknames. For at least two quarters after the fire I was respectfully known as, "Lee the Torch!"

"Would you believe it?" Tom asked Bob, "Riordan actually makes money off these dates."

Bob looked incredulous. "What kind of guy are you anyway, Riordan?"

Tom, Bob and I were on our way to pick up the young ladies who had invited us to their sorority dinner dance. I flicked some imaginary lint off the sleeve of my Tony Martin dinner jacket and sighed. "Gentlemen, gentlemen, these reports are highly exaggerated. The happiness of my date is always my primary concern."

"Yeah, you must be a real cheapie," countered Bob, "what kind of flower did you get?" We were each armed with the mandatory florist's box, containing the mandatory corsage.

"I'll bet it's one of those crummy Hawaiian dandelions," said Bob.

"Gentlemen, you may look forward to observing the affectionate response of my Aphrodite when she gazes on three orchids."

"Three orchids!" they responded in unison. "You're a real bullshitter."

"Please," I said, "I do object to profanity, especially from a pair of cretins."

These two, of course, had bought their corsages in Evanston, a very expensive town. They didn't know of my cut-rate florist, who usually sold flowers outside, under the El tracks on Howard Street, in Chicago. My really big corsage cost much less than their standard flowers.

When we arrived at the sorority house, my date was suitably impressed. "Oh Lee, I don't believe it. Three orchids!" She flung her arms around my neck and kissed me on the mouth - in front of her sorority sisters, the housemother, Tom and Bob - she kissed me on the mouth!

My libido surged, but I quickly remembered we were at Northwestern University. This no doubt would be our most passionate moment of the night.

When we were outside, she whispered, "Now, I have something for you," and she discreetly placed in my hand a brightly wrapped little package, tied with a purple ribbon. This was one custom I really appreciated. Inside, I knew, there would be a carefully folded twenty dollar bill.

Just like the "standard" little package with the expected, but very welcome, twenty dollar bill, the party turned out to be the standard sorority dinner dance. Tom, Bob and I "tripled." We and our dates drove to a palatial home for a festive cocktail party. My date was obviously quite proud of her extravagant corsage, and many of her sorority sisters "oooed" and "aaahed" over it.

After one hour or so, we continued on to the country club for drinks and superb food, followed by dancing. My date and I danced rather gingerly because her extra large corsage got in the way. Anyway, Northwestern girls never danced close. Also, like most Northwestern girls, she drank very little.

When we were at the country club entrance waiting for our car after the party, Tom drew me aside and whispered, "Well, how much do you figure you made tonight?"

"What on earth do you mean?" I answered, looking surprised.

He stared meaningfully at Bob, and then they both shook their heads at me in seeming contempt, as the car arrived.

The next morning, I found I was #9.91 ahead, taking into account what I had spent on the corsage. I went downtown to the second floor of R & K, Evanston's best store for men and made a ten dollar payment on my Tony Martin tuxedo.

While walking down the lushly carpeted stairs to the first floor I spotted Tom and Bob at the shirt counter. A clerk was ringing up their purchases, and they both were about to pay with bills they had just pulled from the brightly wrapped packages they had received from their dates the night before. One still sported its bright purple ribbon.

When they saw me, they tried to do everything but swallow the cute packages. I pretended I didn't see them until I got to the door, where I turned and loudly proclaimed, "You guys sure carry your money in cute little purses!"

One benefit I really appreciated when I made the varsity football team was the clean laundry supplied to me every day. When each one of us arrived at Dyche Stadium for practice we'd go to the equipment-room and be issued a clean tee-shirt, jock strap, silk socks, sweat-socks, and towel. Twice a week we'd get sweat-shirts too. Even though I came from a large high school, this was a luxury I'd never known in athletics before.

After practice we were expected to return each sweaty article to huge designated laundry bags, though many of the guys often kept their tee-shirts, socks and sweat-shirts. Besides the practical aspect of getting some extra clothing, most of us were certain we made a mighty impressive sight strolling the campus clad in tee or sweat shirts stenciled with "Northwestern University Football" across the chest.

At first I resisted the temptation even though most of the

other guys simply borrowed the stuff and eventually returned it. But, I soon fell under the "everyone is doing it" syndrome. I was firmly convinced I really looked super, muscles bulging under one of those "special" tee-shirts.

Now, one of the first facts an athlete quickly learned was that Northwestern women, unlike those at many other schools, didn't give a darn if you were a football player, wrestler, track-man or sports star of any kind. They were primarily concerned with your brain. Luckily, most of us NU athletes had pretty good brains. Our strong, muscular bodies didn't seem to interest the coeds at all, or if they did, it was way down the list.

We quickly noticed however, they did crave our tee-shirts and sweat-shirts. Every gal on campus coveted one. Even a couple of sorority house-mothers confessed how they longed to see one of them carefully folded in their dressers.

What an opportunity! Apparently, the girls had set up an order of desirability. "Northwestern University Football" was first, followed by "Wrestler," the possible double-entendre may have appealed to their baser instincts; then came "Basketball," "Track" and "Cross-Country." Hurray! "Football" was number one, as it should be. Soon the return bags for tee-shirts and sweat-shirts were nearly empty after practice.

We found that most of those gorgeous coeds would go to almost any lengths to obtain a football shirt, and we stocked up. A sweat-shirt, on which the stencilling was particularly clear and unsmudged was good for a sisterly peck on your cheek. A tee-shirt could be counted on to earn a firm, and somewhat friendly handshake. Our team of "Wildcats" was really wild over what we considered these brazen sexual conquests.

Oh sure, the equipment managers noticed. We had four team meetings where the coaches asked, then pleaded with us to stop. But these were not a deterrent. Sex had reared its ugly head, and tired as we usually were, we continued its eager slaves.

The University Fathers declared an emergency. Something had to be done, short of causing the athletes to stink up stadium. Their solution was far crueler. A couple of weeks later in place of those beautiful words "Northwestern University Football" there were three sloppily hand painted Xes across our fronts. They looked awful, actually hideous. No self-respecting sorority girl would even glance at these defiled shirts. Blatent sex for us athletes vanished as if it had never existed. This shock to our systems affected our football team so much we went to the Rose Bowl, and won.

I'll always recall this as one of the most memorable events of my college life. Why did the girls go so crazy for those shirts? I guess they were just a bunch of beautiful women, who wanted to be distinctive.

Yes, but I loved them all. I still do.

What, a wave of creeping nostalgia? I'm too young for this. I get up and stare in the mirror. Outside of a line or two, I don't look much different from how I did in school. I've hardly gained a pound. My sweat-shirt with "Northwestern University Football"

stenciled on the front still fits
like it used to. So do the other
ones in the fourth drawer of my
dresser. Of course the tee-shirts
are beginning to fade a bit, but I
wear them a lot.

Joan asked me to spend the weekend with her. She suggested that we include Friday night, Saturday, Sunday, and return to the campus Monday morning in time for classes. She was fun and extremely attractive. I could hardly believe my good fortune.

While I was excited, both mentally and physically, I quickly realized when a Northwestern coed asked you for the weekend this meant at her home, with live in Mother, Dad and various siblings.

Still, I harbored lustful feelings within my deprived body as we drove her car to a small but fashionable town just across the Wisconsin border. The family home was huge, and her folks friendly even if their greeting seemed slightly tinged with suspicion. I hoped they couldn't sense my desire for their daughter. Her younger brother didn't help by shaking my hand and asking when his sister and I were going to start necking.

Perhaps that's why her Mother stayed up until I was safely

stashed in one of the six upstairs bedrooms.

It looked as if we weren't going anywhere unchaperoned.

But, after a generous breakfast next morning, Joan and I went off to see the town. She asked me to wear my letter sweater.

I felt happy and proud to, of course, but I soon realized she was sort of showing me off. When we were in the grocery store, the bakery, the hardware and the drugstore, she took my hand in a mildly romantic gesture and stood quite close. The young druggist was obviously attracted to her, he seemed reluctant to shake my other hand, and keenly observed how we entwined our fingers and touched.

Did I mind? Well no, especially since I thought that she was getting a bit excited by all this touching, and her warmth and perfume were really getting to me. Her folks took us to the country club for dinner, a delightful experience with plenty of rich food and spirited conversation. But, they watched us like hawks after we returned home.

Around six the next morning I awakened filled with lust. I had just dreamed of "taking" Joan on the plush carpet in front of the downstairs fireplace. Now, I thought of her lush body only a few feet away. But, which bedroom was hers? Might it be worth any risk?

Suddenly, there came a light tapping at my bedroom door. Had I imagined it? No, there it was again.

Instantly, I felt wild with excitement. She was beautiful. The bed large and comfortable. What wondrous circumstances under which to lose my virginity. Too excited to speak, or even whisper, I simply coughed twice.

My bedroom door clicked, and slowly opened. There was Joan in a loosely belted dressing gown that showed plenty. She slowly entered with a finger to her lips entreating my silence. Even though I felt half-crazed I wasn't going to blow this opportunity. I didn't say anything. She did.

"We'll have to whisper," she said quietly approaching my bed.

"O.K., that's fine," I said, turning down the sheets.

"I don't want to embarrass you"

"No, no," I replied, wanting to reach for the almost completely naked breast I could see as she leaned forward.

She looked gorgeous as she spoke sotto voce. "When you go to the toilet, could you be a little quieter?"

I gulped.

"You see my parents have both mentioned the noise you make, and it bothers them."

I gulped again, this time in disbelief.

"Thanks," she whispered, "it doesn't bother me. You could run some water." Then she quickly withdrew toward the door and blew me a kiss before she closed it behind her.

Although we later had a couple of dates, nothing serious came of us. Yet, we always remained friends.

Joan was a valued addition to my Northwestern education. To this day, whenever I go to the toilet for whatever reason, I never fail to run some water.

Our school-year was divided into three quarters, Fall, Winter, and Spring. Because football was so demanding of time and energy, most of the players took the minimum 12 credits in the Fall, and made up for it during the Winter or Spring.

One Spring quarter, I found myself taking six subjects that amounted to a total of 20 credits. It was absolute madness. I handled five of the courses, however, the last which required the reading of seven books I had to let slide.

The night before the final exam, I tried to scan the seven books. This was a literature course, and I'd read four of the books in high school, but I didn't seem to remember much about any one of them. The scanning served to confuse me, and I looked upon the task as impossible, pretty hopeless.

I decided to trust to blind luck. I carefully read one chapter from each of the seven volumes. About 4:00 a.m., my roommate Tom who was studying for another exam, told me my methods were stupid, but that he admired me. He did, I'll admit, try to lift my spirits:

"Tomorrow, at 8:00 a.m. you will represent a Northwestern man during his finest hour -- when he walks into an exam chest out, head held high, knowing full-well he's going to flunk it cold and add a sure 'F' on his transcript."

He affectionately grabbed my shoulder. "You my boy will be a hero, another purple legend."

His words were hardly reassuring.

At 7:50, clad in my army fatigues, I arrived at the exam room, ready to become, as Tom had put it, "another purple legend." <u>I'm going to flunk this cold</u>.

There were seven essay questions, a fact I noticed immediately, but I read only the first one so as not to panic. It was somewhat general, however, it concentrated on the chapter I had worked on so diligently.

The second also concentrated on the chapter I'd read carefully. I couldn't believe my luck.

The same situation prevailed for the third, but there were four more. Number four was on the chapter I'd read, too. So were the questions on book five, book six, and even book seven, the largest of the lot.

Oh sure, my literary background helped, as did the fact that I'd read some of the volumes in high school years before, but by a stroke of unbelievable luck, I'd picked seven "winners" in a row.

My roomie Tom was very impressed. With all our exams over the next day he took me to the horse races, a sport that interested him.

"I've dreamed of meeting a guy like you," he said handing me a sheet with horses names. "Think about it and pick the winners."

He lost over $100 bucks. I picked the horse that finished dead last in each of ten races.

"You can make at least fifty bucks a night," one of the guys on the wrestling team told me. He was referring to the possibility of my becoming a part-time professional wrestler.

The pay sounded great as I seemed always short of money at school. Fifty bucks was a fortune. I could wrestle, and had a good heavy build coupled with a muscular body.

I went to the arena one afternoon for an interview with Mr. Hollywood the wrestling impressario. He sat hunched over his desk smoking a vile cigar. It wasn't like talking with a Northwestern professor, but he appeared a surprisingly compassionate man.

"So you need bucks?"

"Yessir."

"So, let's see it," he ordered flicking ashes.

"See what?"

"The bod kid. Strip to your shorts."

"But, I can wrestle," I protested.

"Don't make no difference. The bod kid."

I stripped to my shorts, feeling somewhat embarrassed.

He got out of his chair and studied me from behind his desk. "You could do, kid. The ladies'll like your bod. Now, show me pain."

"What?"

"Let's see pain on your face." He puffed on his cigar. "Some guy has just kicked you in the stones. Let's see pain on your face."

I created my quickest painful expression.

"Good, good. Now show me mad. Some guy just pinched your girl's ass. Let's see mad."

I stomped around his office roaring mad.

"Good, good, kid. You just might work out O.K. Put your clothes on. I'll tell you what. I'll try you with "Gypsy George" in a prelim Thursday night. Be here at 6:30."

"Gee, thanks," I said.

He smiled somewhat paternally. "Fifty bucks if I use you, and you take care of any doctor bills."

"Is it that dangerous?" I asked stupidly.

He snorted, "You got more chance of getting hurt crossing Western Avenue."

After I left his office I thought my experience in University Theater might come in handy.

Thursday night I became acquainted with one of the nicest guys I'd ever met, Gypsy George. He was dubbed the "Croatian Killer" even though his heritage was Greek. I learned a great deal quickly from George, including the fact that he drove a garbage truck in Chicago.

"This is sort of like a dance, with a few hard bumps," he explained, "we try to plan what we're going to do." He and I choreographed our most important moves. "The main thing to remember," he declared shaking his finger at me, "don't hurt nobody."

He continued to instruct me in falling on the practice ring located in the basement. When the impressario stopped by, George assured him, "He'll do good, Mr Hollywood."

"I'm glad to hear that," he acknowledged. "You're on first, so give 'em a good show." Hollywood's assistant handed me a cowboy hat that was too small and a "blood capsule" to bite after George "smashed" me in the face, half-way through the bout. "Remember," warned Hollywood, "you guys go a half hour max!"

"O.K. Mr Hollywood," answered George respectfully. Then we went into more rehearsal.

Promptly at 8 o'clock we trotted into the packed arena, from opposite sides. The crowd roared. George wore a yellow and black satin robe over his large, but flabby frame. On the back the words "Croatian Killer" blazed forth. My white terry cloth robe didn't impress anyone, even topped by my cowboy hat.

Because George had explained so thoroughly, it didn't surprise me when the crowd booed his introduction, and roundly cheered that of the "Wichita Kid." I had to hold my hat on when I stepped to the middle of the ring as the multitude cheered louder. Perhaps, it was my purple tights.

193

No, as George had pointed out, He'd obviously be the bad guy, older, long-haired, sloppily overweight; while I'd be the good guy, young, nice looking, with a trim, muscled body. While I stood in mid-ring for my introduction, George spat at me.

Our match went along pretty much as rehearsed. My opponent constantly "fouled" me with groin kicks, eye rips, choke holds, and a knee-drop to the head as I rolled on the mat in supposed agony after he'd dragged my eyes across the ring turnbuckles. Of course, I screamed and stumbled around the ring until he body-slammed me. The "referee" consistently warned George. He "punched" the ref, too.

George was awarded a "near fall" for the knee-drop. He was awarded another one after a "dirty" elbow smash felled me to the canvas. When I got up, I bit the blood capsule so crimson gore gouted from my lips, over both of us and onto the ring. The crowd screamed. There were calls of "hang in there kid." "He's a dirty fighter, kid." "Do something ref!"

One fact really surprised me, the large proportion of women in the audience. They yelled the loudest, and naturally most of them were on my side. They sure gave it to George. "You fat greasy pig!" "You rotten slime, why don't you fight fair?" "You're cute." "Go get 'im kid."

It really was time to "get him." In a clinch, George grunted "five minutes, kid." Finally, after taking twenty minutes of "punishment" it was time for the "good guy" to come back. As I began to have the better of it, the crowd went insane. Even I got excited!

I bounced off the ropes, took him down with a block, and got an easy bar-arm. His face contorted and he shrieked in pain. He was so good I felt actually afraid I'd hurt him.

Always considerate, he winked at me. I got him in a step-over toe-hold and then flopped sort of on him in a crotch-hold. He struggled, however to no avail and the referee signaled a pin. The arena went berserk.

Mr. Hollywood appeared pleased when he handed me my 50 dollars. "You did good kid, real good."

"I told you he would, Mr. Hollywood." chortled George.

"You were right," agreed the impressario. he peeled three twenties off his roll, thought about it for a couple of seconds, peeled off another one and handed the four to the Croatian Killer. Then he looked at me. "Someday you'll make money like that -- maybe -- huh, kid?"

Pretty soon I was getting a couple of matches per week and even advanced to three once in awhile. As the popular "good guy" the Wichita Kid, I faced some of the wrestlers with "really bad" reputations. As a group, they were probably one of the nicest bunches of men I ever knew.

I even got to face one of those with the "meanest" reputation, "Monster Man Montezuma," from Guadalajara, Mexico. Actually, he liked to be called "Donald," had seven children, and an extensive milk delivery route in Chicago. Don, or Donald and I practiced and rehearsed the "dirty tricks" he

196

used on me. They were really effective before an emotional audience which always cheered for me, playing the good guy.

Now, I trotted to the ring wearing my hat and old robe with the legend "Wichita Kid" on the back. I blew kisses to the ladies, who stood, squealed, and blew them back. The only reaction of derision came from a few Fraternity Brothers, who dropped in, now and then to see the fun and give me the razzberry. Of course, I loved seeing them in the crowd.

Monster Man Montezuma and I met weekly for a series of matches. The impressario even considered letting M.M.M. win one, but eventually decided against the idea because he didn't think the crowd would stand for it. Why tamper with a good thing reasoned Mr. Hollywood.

Monster Man began his intimidation even before he got in the ring. Wearing a huge fake Aztec headdress and a wildly colored satin robe, he screamed a few spanish phrases he'd memorized at members of the audience who jeered him. Uniformed "security" men often had to restrain him from tearing a spectator apart.

Actually, his exuberance carried over into our matches, and he hurt me slightly a few times. I never forgot he had seven kids. Besides, he always apologized. How the crowd loved to boo and curse him.

We added a few extras to our repertoire of tricks. I usually had two blood capsules to chomp on when "smashed" in the face on separate occasions. I was afraid I'd choke on or swallow them. So, we arranged for a "security" man to secretly hand me the second when I jumped out of the ring, a skulking coward, to avoid being mashed by a mad Montezuma.

Donald would claw at the referee, who kept warning him to stop his "dirty" tricks. In the process of clawing at him, he'd tear his shirt, and as the ref adjusted his garment over his head and couldn't see, Donald would pull a coat hanger out of his tights and bend it around my neck. While I flopped all over the ring fighting for air the audience often had to be restrained from coming to my rescue.

Another extra had the same "security" man sneaking me some corn kernels, which I'd ceremoniously spit out after a particularly vicious smash to the mouth. They were supposed to be teeth and the crowd close to ringside bought it all the way. Happily, I continued to be able to smile at the friendly crowd, showing my own teeth, week after week. Of course, I was the good guy, who took the "beating," but always managed to pin the evil Monster Man right at the end. The packed house loved it.

By now, I made 70 dollars for each performance, and I was about to become part of a huge promotion. Three of us gladiators would be formed into a tag-team to face the "German Blimp." One man would not be enough to face the Teutonic air bag because he weighed over 500 pounds. Supposedly, he had destroyed all opponents in this country and on the continent. Those he'd rolled over on never had wrestled again. Posters sprang up everywhere announcing his one night appearance. At hugely elevated ticket prices with only reserved seating. There were even a couple of radio spots.

A poster that caught my eye stated there'd be clergymen ringside to administer last rites to his vanquished opponents. The words "if necessary" were included, too. I felt uncertain as to whether or not I wanted to share the ring with the Blimp.

Mr. Hollywood almost shook with excitement. The arena sold out over two weeks before the match. He promised me and my tag team partners, now billed as the "Windy City Three," 100 dollars each, plus a bonus if we put on an especially "good show." We didn't know if that included getting squashed and perhaps the "last rites."

Both George and Donald advised me to "stay out of this one." They wanted no part of his 500 plus pounds. They also pointed out there wouldn't be any rehearsal to choreograph the show. The Blimp always refused rehearsal. "What is this setup?" queried George. "This guy may be for real!"

Neither I nor my partners in the Windy City Three withdrew. I felt stupid, but curious too.

When I saw the German Blimp on the big night, I recalled how "curiosity" had "killed the cat." While we waited in the basement I tried to speak German to him. He only grunted and roared. I didn't think he knew any German, but he sure was a "Blimp," and I bet he weighed closer to 700. He lay on a floor mat because there wasn't any piece of furniture large enough to support him. Every once in awhile he'd beat his massive fists on his completely bald head. Then he'd roar.

Our trio entered the standing room only arena on the opposite side from the Blimp. he didn't walk, but rather oozed down his aisle. A small band played German martial music. I felt real scared. So did my partners. "What if he rolls over on you?" Yah right! What if?!!

We grabbed the ring ropes and tumbled onto the canvas, then stood up joining arms. It was impressive, but we weren't feeling impressive. I hoped our fright wouldn't show. We were cheered.

At least a dozen big guys pushed and shoved the Blimp into the ring, bending a ring-post outward in the process. They shoved him toward the middle. The band struck up Deutshland Uber Alles which I thought was a bit too much. Anyway, there were many more boos than cheers.

Standing at mid-ring the German Blimp resumed pounding his head with his massive fists. He slowly lifted his right foot, let it hang there a moment, and slammed it down.

Crash! It was like a thunderous earthquake. The middle of the ring collapsed. His "German majesty "was up to his armpits. He flailed and roared like a stricken animal but he was trapped. A hundred men, including the three of us couldn't budge him. Two hundred men, including the three of us couldn't budge him.

None of the crowd left. They seemed to love the drama of the situation. A thunderous ovation greeted the Chicago Fire Department. The firefighters stood around shaking their collective heads. We went downstairs and dressed in our street clothes.

A few minutes later we three were drinking beer in a nearby tavern. While drinking beers one through six, we admitted we'd been pretty scared. While drinking beers seven through ten, we were sure we could have taken the Blimp.

When we wobbled past the arena, there were hundreds of people standing outside, but we didn't go in. The fire trucks were still there, and we could hear the sound of axes chopping on wood.

Funny, although I considered it I never did try to collect that 100 dollars from Mr. Hollywood.

About the closest most of us got to sex at Northwestern was taking the course "Marriage and the Family." Hardly anyone ever cut that class, and many people who were not even registered used to sit in on the lectures.

One lecture concentrated on how babies were made. You could have heard the proverbial pin drop. Our professor revealed a startling fact. "It's really amazing that there are so many people in the world. A great multitude of optimum conditions must prevail. The truth is, it's very difficult to make a baby." At that bit of news, the entire class got to its feet applauding and cheering.

Another class took place where students stood and applauded. Strangely enough, the overall subject was political science and Norris Fester and I were both in it. While wandering off his original subject, our professor expressed the opinion that if not engaged in to excess, premarital sex was acceptable. Instantly these class members were on their feet cheering. The Professor's face got red.

His remark was carefully noted by the ever astute Fester. "You know he's got a daughter in school here?"

"No, I didn't. So what?"

"So what?' he shot back as though I were a supremely idiotic moron. "Her old man says sex is O.K. It's likely she feels the same way."

He called her. She said she didn't know Norris. She also said for some reason a lot of guys she didn't know were calling her up and asking for dates. When necessary, Fester could be quite charming. She finally agreed to meet him at Cooley's Cupboard for a caramel roll and hot chocolate.

"Wow, Norris, you're really making progress," I kidded him, "a caramel roll and hot chocolate!"

"These things take time," he noted confidently.

Actually, we were both so inexperienced, neither one of us knew if "these things took time" or not.

But, he continued seeing her, subtly indicating that their dates were getting warmer and warmer. "She says she sincerely likes me." He bought her discreet presents. No doubt, he was moving in.

Eventually, all their dates ended up at The Little Esquire ice cream shop. Often, I was asked along, with or without a date. Fester wanted company.

I asked him what had gone wrong? Why wasn't he moving in any more?

He settled back in a chair and sighed. "Well, I analyzed the situation carefully. I've got a big advantage because I live at home."

"Sure, sure Fester, go on."

"So, what if she says, Norris, I want to have sex with you. My analysis tells me these facts. My folks are going to be home for at least two months. We go to my Fraternity House, and we can't go above the first floor. We go to her Sorority House and we can't go above the first floor. We sit in my car on campus and a watchman shines his flashlight over us. We sit in my car off campus and an Evanston policeman shines his flashlight over us.

"If we try to register at the Orrington Hotel they'll want to see a marriage license or wedding rings because we look like students. It'd be the same at the North Shore Hotel. If we start to make out in the grass along the lake the Evanston Police will sweep through with their phalanx of motorcycles with spotlights, every hour."

"Yeh," I agreed. "I've seen them work their motorcycles wedge. I was sitting alone on a bench near the lake and they stopped and indicated I was some kind of weirdo."

"Sure," said Fester, "they like to "shave" bodies with their wheels."

"Yeh," I agreed again, "I've seen 'em in action."

"So, I've come to the conclusion," he leaned forward to emphasize his point, "after much deliberation, that sex is impossible here at Northwestern."

"Yeh," I agreed yet again, "I think you're right."

"You know I'm right!" Now he settled back as though content that he'd made his point. For the second time he sighed. "We both know I'm right."

We maintained silence for a few minutes, each deep in his own thoughts, his own personal problems.

"Say Norris," I ventured, "you might like this class of mine called 'Marriage and the Family.' We could go together. You don't even have to be registered."

"Oh sure, I've heard about it," he acknowledged. "Lots of talk about sex and stuff like that. Doesn't it meet at 10:30?"

"That's right!" I smiled somewhat patronizingly. "Monday, Wednesday and Friday. Norris, you're going to love it."

The Friday before Exam Week, all over the campus, signs sprang up declaring, "Exam Week Is Hell," and no matter how well you kept up with your courses it always turned out to be just that, "hell." We faced this hell three times per year because Northwestern operated on the quarterly system.

People went berserk as The Week approached, and got steadily crazier as it progressed. Most carried four subjects, which meant four exams. There simply weren't any "snap courses." Your professor could ask anything - our teachers always upheld N.U.'s reputation for academic toughness - so you had to study and review everything.

Guys didn't shave, bathe or sleep very much. They wore jeans or fatigues and sweat shirts to exams, the girls did too. Nobody would be caught dead dressed like that for regular classes.

Before the week actually commenced, students tried to do something unusual to distract themselves from the reality lurking only a short time away. We always found something to take our minds off the impending week of hell.

This particular Saturday night was no exception. Our Housemother had left for the weekend, visiting her grown children. Hank our President, the future Jeffrey Hunter of the movies, was attending a conference at the University of Chicago. The time seemed right for deviltry, but what?

The idea came in a strange and singularly unattractive form. A short time before dinner Okie walked down the third floor hall naked. Someone shouted "Okie, can't you put something on? Every time I see you nude, I want to throw up."

Okie was used to these gibes, because he had been cursed into a body that looked like an emaciated scarecrow with knobs at every joint. But, he had his pride. "I'm going down to dinner this way, and no one's going to stop me."

We normally dressed for dinner, ties, shirts, coats, the works. Perhaps, it was only natural Okie's idea or threat, took hold as a brief rebellion against our usual decorum. "Hey, let's all go to dinner - naked!"

Shouts of "nude, nude, nude, nude!" echoed through our House. It swept like a prairie fire right up until the dinner bell rang.

In a few minutes, some seventy Brothers were seated in the dining room waiting to be served. All of them were naked. Even the waiters were without a stitch.

Someone had substituted for me on the board-job. As Vice-President, being the highest ranking officer present, I sat at the head table, where our Housemother and President usually sat, nearest the door.

I felt a little strange leading grace, under the circumstances, but reasoned that the fact of the nude assembly should not alter our thanks for the meal. Besides, I could lead our group in grace while seated.

Dinner went as usual, perhaps with a bit more laughter and a higher level of jocularity. Nobody even mentioned we were all in our birthday suits. I didn't overhear a single joke about our condition.

Just before dessert was served the dining room door opened and there stood our President in a blue suit, with a lovely young lady on his arm. Luckily the waiters were in the kitchen. Instantly, the room became completely silent.

"Ah, Lee, where's Mrs. Joss?" he asked.

I realized he must have assumed we were eating without our shirts. "Ah, Hank, she's away for the weekend." The silence continued.

"Lavinia Smith is from the University of Chicago," he announced to the seated group, "I wanted to show her the finest Fraternity at Northwestern.

Finally the foreboding silence was broken with tumultuous and lengthy applause. During the applause, I could tell Hank had recognized the overall situation. He didn't panic.

I tapped my water glass with a spoon asking for quiet. Eventually it came.

"Welcome to you Lavinia Smith. Welcome from the members of the finest Fraternity on campus." I paused, clearing my throat. "We are gentlemen, each and everyone of us.

And, we all know, when a gentleman sees a lady enter the room, he gets up to his feet."

Hank grabbed her hand. "Don't you dare!" he shouted, and out the door they went, and quickly down the hall.

Northwestern has always been well-known for its academic excellence. It follows that the competition for grades was fierce, and all the courses tough.

Since we operated on a three quarter schedule for the usual academic year, instead of two semesters we really had to study hard. In just a few weeks, you were facing final exams, and you could count on them being really difficult.

I well remember my most traumatic exam, because I almost "died" while taking it. I shook for hours after I finished.

The course covered advance mathematics, and in order to do the problems you had to utilize one of over thirty possible formulas and consult math tables that were in the back of the textbook.

Now, my fraternity brothers and I, like our fellow students, were pretty astute. The test would be hard enough even though of the "open-book" variety. Why not write the formulas in among the tables and save the awful trouble of memorizing them?

Two of the four of us who were to face the exam decided to take a chance and write the formulas in the book. I decided to try to memorize them. What a task! I almost opted for stashing the formulas too.

On the morning of the two hour final those who wrote among the math tables decided to erase the formulas. We'd try to rely on our failing memories. And, quite luckily,too.

Before our Professor passed out the exam problems, he moved around the small class and quickly checked each student's book, searching for written formulas. He didn't find any. It had been a close call for my friends and would have meant an automatic "F for cause."

Wow, the exam was tough, and while I congratulated myself on not cheating on the formulas, I had a terrible time remembering them. They were a morass in my mixed mind, and at times I simply stared around the room trying to collect my wits.

My eyes strayed to Daphne who was seated behind me in the row to my left. A real doll, she was dressed in blue and intermittently lifted her blue skirt. It took me awhile to realize that she had the formulas on the insides of her thighs; half on the left and half on the right. A terrible distraction.

This drove me crazy of course, and I tried energetically to read the formulas on her luscious flesh. As the exam progressed she raised her skirt higher and higher. I found the stupid theory that coeds never wore panties to be untrue.

I think our Professor knew what she was up to, but there wasn't much he could do about it. He would have created a real scandal by asking her to lift her skirt so he could examine the inside of her thighs.

The two hour exam passed all too quickly. I was a mess at the end. I think I felt in love with Daphne.

Out in the hall, most of us exhaustedly compared notes.

She asked, "How did you do, Lee?"

"I think I flunked," I replied, "but I love your panties."

She flushed, "Women have to have some advantages." She walked away in a huff.

I got the lowest grade of my university career.

Daphne received an "A."

MY CLEANEST QUARTER

On the second floor of our House, there was a milk cooler where you could buy a pint of regular or chocolate milk on the honor system. You simply signed your name on a sheet attached to the cooler and were billed for your purchases at the end of the quarter. One of the Brothers, who needed some extra money, ran the popular concession. The system worked quite well until Norris Fester began signing my name.

It wasn't a matter of money where Norris was concerned, he only did it as a joke, and to get the better of me. He always had a ravenous appetite and he never drank fewer than four pints of milk at a time. I drank a few pints myself.

How to stop Fester? I wracked my brain. How to get the better of him?

Another concession ran on a weekly basis. It consisted of laundry and dry cleaning. I usually mailed my laundry home like most everyone else, but I decided to give my mother a rest and let Fester do it. He wouldn't know about it, at least temporarily. I also determined to let him take care of my cleaning, by putting his name on tags in my slacks, coats, jackets, etc., etc.

At the end of each quarter a day was designated on which the Brothers paid up for the various services they had used over the past busy months. This time I really dressed up for "the day" in a perfectly pressed suit, crisply clean shirt and tie.

I paid my astronomical milk bill which was at least partially mine. Norris paid a small amount because he had mistakenly signed his own name a few times. He was putting his wallet back when the Treasurer asked, "How about your cleaning and laundry bill, Norris?"

"Wadda you mean?" he asked astonished, "I don't even live in the House!"

"Well, I've got bills for you," asserted the Treasurer. "They come to $56.70."

"What? I never had any laundry or cleaning done."

219

At that moment, I walked up. "Fester, you trying to work some scam, again? Why not make a clean breast of it and pay up?"

He looked at me glumly. "No wonder you're so cleaned and pressed, like you came out of the pages of Esquire Magazine."

"Well, Norris I turned over a new leaf this quarter."

"And it's going to cost me $56.70."

The Treasurer was becoming impatient. "Norris will you pay this by check or do you have the cash?"

He paid by check.

He turned to me with a benign look on his face and asked, "care for a chocolate milk?"

"Sure."

He removed two pints, handed me one and signed the list. It read "Norris Fester."

"You know, Fester," I said taking a satisfying gulp of chocolate milk. "Things are always more enjoyable when someone else buys."

The Assistant Athletic Director took a minute to light his cigar, dragged on it furiously, blew a strangling cloud in my direction, and tipped back in his chair. "Did you ever hear of Alan Ameche?"

I tried to keep from coughing as I thought about the name. "Well, no I don't think so." I couldn't resist a wisecrack, "I've heard of Don Ameche. He invented the telephone didn't he?"

The AAD was in no mood for levity. "You're a real comedian, Riordan. Sometimes I think we keep you around here just for laughs."

"Well, no sir, I honestly haven't heard about this particular Ameche."

He leaned forward and pointed his cigar at me like a loaded pistol. "He's an All-State Fullback from Kenosha High School, and he wants to come here to Northwestern. He's going to look us over this weekend, and your job is to keep him happy, and to make a good impression for your school."

Since I was the recipient of an athletic scholarship, I immediately understood my responsibility in this matter. "I suppose you picked me because I'm from Wisconsin, too."

"Yeah, you got the idea," he replied, puffing away, "besides you're pretty good on the football field, and you aren't too rough around the edges."

The next Friday evening I met Ameche's train. He really seemed interested in becoming a Wildcat.

He stayed at my Fraternity House. Al seemed to be a nice, rather bright young fellow and obviously a hot football prospect.

I did my best, showed him around our outstanding campus, spending extra time on the athletic facilities; introduced him to girls and guys. I even took him to Chicago, but I tried not to oversell the entire picture. Later he even admitted to me he actually was a shirt-tail relative of Don Ameche.

On Sunday morning we went to church and then returned to the House for a delicious brunch. Al confided to me that he wanted Northwestern more than any other school. I was happy. I told him the truth, "I love this place." He said he could see why I did.

We arrived on time for his two o'clock appointment with the Assistant Athletic Director. I felt worried. In those days, a high school senior had to negotiate the best deal he could, at any big-time football school.

The AAD, complete with his cigar, met us in Patton Gym. I remained outside the office because the "deals" were always confidential, and because I felt I should take Al to meet his train home.

I tried to hear what was going on in the office. The voices became louder and louder, and soon I could catch a few words. Apparently, the deal was not up to Ameche's expectations.

After about an hour, he and the AAD emerged. The big fullback from Kenosha looked disappointed. The Assistant Athletic Director patted Al on the back and said, "Remember Al, fullbacks like you are a dime a dozen at Northwestern."

On the way to his, train, Al told me he felt hurt and mad. I told him I was pretty unhappy, too. When the train arrived, we shook hands as friends.

Two years later, I sat in the stands watching Ameche go 76 yards on the first play from scrimmage as Wisconsin buried Northwestern.

In another year, it was "Alan Ameche, All-American." Later, he set many rushing records with the Baltimore Colts. Then he became, "Alan Ameche, All Pro Fullback."

I've often wondered over the years how many times he recalled those parting words, "Remember Al, fullbacks like you are a dime a dozen......."

Two squads of Evanston Police leaped on their waiting motorcycles and cranked those Harleys to a roar when they saw the Lincoln convertible turn into their street. Uniforms immaculate, boots glistening, they formed a double phalanx, a guard of honor to clear the way for one of America's greatest heroes.

Perhaps these Evanston officers should have been surprised when the black limosine arrived six and one-half minutes early. If any one of them had looked carefully, he might have noted that the wired flags on each fender had a row of four stars instead of a circle of five. And, surely every one of these cops would have been stupified if he'd examined the driver, and the dignified personage sitting casually in the rear seat, dressed in a trench-coat, scarf and khaki military cap, wearing aviator sun-glasses, with an unlit corn-cob pipe clenched in his chattering teeth.

On this morning of April 27, 1951, those Evanston policemen must have felt proud to be the escort of General Douglas MacArthur. Fortunately, they did not know the driver of the Lincoln convertible usually answered to the name of Norris Fester, and the creature impersonating "The General"- was I.

Yes, my teeth were chattering as they gripped the pipe, not because I felt cold, but because I was scared....., absolutely terrified.

When we had invaded the Glenview Naval Air Station, I remembered almost defecating. But, this was worse, riding in full view of thousands of people, any one of whom might notice we weren't quite up to regulation. Yelling his suspicions at us imposters, could alert the police who were now holding back the crowd in this most populous part of Evanston. I knew I'd be constipated for a week, if we lived.

The day before, I'd worked on an NBC television crew (part of Northwestern Communications School training) while three million people welcomed MacArthur to

Chicago. I remembered the great "shots" we got of Mrs. MacArthur's car, completely covered with 1,000 orchids donated by a Loop florist.

That night it had been announced that the General would leave the Stevens Hotel at exactly 7:30 a.m. the next morning and be conducted by the Chicago Mayor to the south limits of Evanston. MacArthur's eventual destination, after riding up the north shore, was revealed as Milwaukee.

When I returned to the campus after my television stint, and told these details to Norris Fester, he almost went out of his head. "Man, this is our greatest opportunity. No one - absolutely no one will ever forget this caper. We'll be famous."

"You're insane, Norris. Count me out of any more crazy stunts."

He faced me and stared purposely, "And, it's being handed right to us on a platter." He began pacing. "On a platter - right on a platter." He paused for a moment, his eyes blazing, "After tomorrow - we'll both be immortal."

Now, it may seem strange in the light of the next day's events, but

227

we both fervently admired Douglas MacArthur. We felt he was a hero and had nothing against him. It just happened the General would be in the right place at the right time - to challenge Fester's warped ingenuity. And, Norris had the equipment to take advantage of the circumstances - his father's Lincoln convert, the general's four-starred flags, a huge supply of intestinal fortitude, access to an impressive uniform, and a gutless co-conspirator to wear the uniform, me.

He gleefully outlined his plan, or as he referred to it, "Operation Doug." I repeatedly protested, "No, no Norris. I'm out of it. Forget it. I won't do it!" He, of course, ignored me, becoming more enthusiastic as each detail fell into place.

"And, the street layout is perfect, absolutely perfect."

"No Fester, I won't do it. I've gone along with you before, but this is impossible. You're insane. Nuts!" I reached for a cigarette. Neither of us smoked.

"When Doug gets to the Chicago city limits, he'll have to turn 90o hard-right to enter Evanston," Fester exhulted. The Chicago escort will have to drop him just before the turn, and the Evanston Police will pick him up right after it."

"But, what if," I took a long drag on the cigarette, "what if the two escorts meet, with us in the middle?"

Norris laughed, as though at my stupidity. "They won't, we'll have cleared the Evanston Police out with us. They can't see around the corner because of the apartments. They'll have to assume we're the real thing."

"Dammit Fester. I won't do it!"

"There'll be the entire University out there when we drive past. We'll live in their memories forever. We'll be immortal - our finest stunt - absolutely immortal!"

The cigarette I'd been dragging on so furiously burned my fingers. "Ouch," I yelled angrily. "It's too risky and it can't work. Count me out, Fester!"

As we moved rapidly northward on Sheridan Road, still well south of the campus, people began edging out into the street.

"Way to go, General."

"Tell Truman to stuff it!"

I waved to the admirers, but didn't smile. I also saluted quite often. Somehow, even with the glasses and the corn-cob pipe, I felt my profile was wrong.

A couple of roses landed in the back seat. Our pace quickened and the Police turned on their sirens. The second rank of motorcycles closed around our convertible. _Geez_, I wondered, _how much farther before we're discovered? Someone out there must have served with the General_. I seemed to recall movies showing crowds tearing infidels apart. Could it happen in Evanston, Illinois? We'd probably find out.

If Norris were nervous, he certainly didn't appear so from behind. Surrounded by all that noise, we couldn't possibly talk, and it wouldn't look right for him to turn and gaze or wink at such a supreme personage. I thought, _what if we have a flat?_

By the time we reached the south end of the campus, our entourage was moving at about 35 miles an hour. Would anyone recognize us? I pulled up the collar of my trench-coat. A bouquet bounced off Fester's head and tangled in an escorting motorcycle. Then a regular barrage of flowers swept over us, but most missed falling into the car because of our speed. A single rose stabbed me through my glove.

Suddenly, we slowed, almost stopped. Eight-thirty classes had been delayed, so, at the curve near Scott Hall Student Union, the cheering crowd was huge. Many pushed forward.

"Hello Doug."

"We love Mac!" a group chanted in unison.

One guy forced his way up to the convertible, thrust out his hand and shouted, "I was in the Philippines, General." I nodded my head, patted his arm and lost my pipe. He seemed satisfied as we slowly moved past him. I searched for my pipe under a deluge of flowers.

My head bumped against the front seat. We'd stopped. I grabbed my military cap, retrieved my pipe and carefully looked around.

"We love Mac!" The chant became a roar.

The police gently held the admirers back. Waving to the throng, I clamped the pipe back in my mouth. There, only a few feet away stood a gorgeous coed I'd dated only last month, staring right at me. I tried to remember if we were still friends. Her lips formed words, I couldn't distinguish. What was she saying? She was repeating, yes, yes, "We love Mac! We love Mac!" Wow, what a relief.

A motorcycle cop hopped off his vehicle, pushed his face close to mine and blurted, "When we get to the city limits, can I have your autograph, General?" He waved some sort of slender volume.

"I never give autographs, son," I proclaimed through clenched teeth. He appeared rather disappointed, but jumped back on his cycle as we began to move again.

Just before the sirens resumed their wail, I distinctly heard someone shout, "Hey, that's Fester and Riordan?" Fester stiffened at the wheel. My eyes rolled around, trying to identify the source of our danger. Thankfully we picked up speed while the sirens shrieked.

The crowds lining Sheridan Road near the main campus saw MacArthur and his escort as an indistinct blur. There were shouts of approval anyway, and a Delta Gamma sorority pin landed in my lap. I was astonished -- A DeeGee pin of my very own! Before it slipped off I grabbed it, and put it in my trench-coat pocket.

We moved swiftly -- swiftly toward the border between Evanston and Wilmette -- where the moment of truth we couldn't face was waiting for us.

Fester often refrained from revealing the most important details of his outlandish plans to me. This time I had no idea how we could escape and avoid at least a prison term. "Holy cow," I mumbled as we slipped by Northwestern's impressive Technological Institute, what kind of sentence will we get for impersonating an American legend? Why hell, it suddenly dawned on me. I'm the one impersonating MacArthur!

There were only a few blocks before Wilmette. I recalled there was a slight jog in the road before the two suburbs met -- I jumped in terror. Norris began blowing the horn repeatedly, then accelerated wildly as the motorcycle. lines parted.

When the Evanston motorcycle police dropped behind, I swiveled around and saluted them energetically. Some waved. A few returned my salute. We moved even faster, our horn constantly blaring. I turned back in my seat and saw the Wilmette Police taking off, jets of smoke streaming from their exhausts -- trying to stay ahead of us.

I hurtled across the rear seat when Fester spun the big convertible hard left into Central Street, accompanied by the sound of tortured rubber. The few spectators in this area must have been surprised, but neither police group could see us, now. Our speedometer hit 60.

Behind a supermarket, we dumped everything -- flags, trench-coat, glasses, cap, etc., etc., into the trunk and grabbed a couple of bags of fine dirt and two wet rags. We poured dirt over the rags and rubbed the convertible's gleaming metal and finished by dirtying the white-sidewall tires. The car looked like it had been out in the country.

"The pipe," said Fester, handing me my books.

"What?" I asked, "you mean the ----"

He yanked the corn-cob pipe out of my mouth and threw it and the rags into the trunk.

Fester left the car on the grease-rack at a nearby service garage where he'd made an appointment.

"Naw, don't wash it - just a lube and an oil change - and maybe you'd better tune it up."

When we returned to the campus, we strolled leisurely along the lake. There weren't any classes scheduled until 9:30.

One of our Fraternity Brothers came walking up, a big grin on his face. "Hey, did you guys see MacArthur?"

"No," I replied, "I wanted to, but I sacked in."

"Yeh," said Fester, "I needed the sleep. How was it?"

235

"Well, it was pretty exciting. Course, he went by fast with the police escort. Big crowd though. Lotsa cheering."

"Geez," I said, "too bad to miss something like that."

"You know," said the Brother with thoughtful emphasis, "something really strange happened. A few minutes after MacArthur went by, another guy came along in a big convertible <u>pretending</u> to be MacArthur."

"What's that?" I said, my voice quavering, "You mean an imposter?"

"Well, of course, but there wasn't any harm done. Hardly anybody even noticed him. Must have been some crazy."

"Yeh," said Fester, nodding, then shaking his head. "These days there sure are a lot of real weirdos around."

"I'll move up on him in the turn and be in front of him just as we hit the home stretch," said Bob pointing to the track diagram.

"Yes," said our track coach nodding, "then you'll take him on the outside Lee. That should give you your best chance."

"It could work," I agreed, "Wow, would I like to finally beat that guy!"

Coach, Bob and I were making plans for Saturday's quadrangular track meet between Indiana, Notre Dame, Purdue and us. The particular event we were talking about was the quarter-mile, a grueling "once around the track." The guy with whom we were concerned was Indiana's Frank Fleetfoot.

The newspapers described the Hoosier star as "a blazing quarter-miler, the best in the Big Ten, and perhaps in the country." Bob, my teammate, was a bit slower than I, so he was going to cut in front of Fleetfoot -- legally of course -- just before the final stretch drive. In theory at least, it might throw the Hoosier a tad off stride. By avoiding the congestion, and coming up with a super finish, I might have a chance to win.

Next day just before the race, I noticed Frank fussing with his shorts. He looked in excellent shape, but unusually nervous. He put his hands inside his crimson top with the big "Indiana" on it and seemed to be stretching it as he inhaled big gulps of air. "Good Luck," he blurted, when in a friendly gesture he grabbed my hand.

"Same to you, Frank," I replied, noticing that both our hands were shaking and wet.

The starter bellowed, "Runners, take your marks." This was a staggered start on the turn, and we'd have to stay in our lanes until the backstretch. There were eight lanes, two for each school. I had number four, Bob three, and Fleetfoot number one. This was good placement for us, but since the Hoosier flyer was inside and to my left, I couldn't see him.

"Get set!" I pulled air into my lungs, lifting my butt simultaneously. I'd try for a rolling start.

BANG

It worked perfectly. A great start! I hit the backstretch in third. Two guys passed me, but I felt good. My stride seemed easy and quick. I knew Frank would lay back as usual, waiting to devour his competitors.

Halfway into the final turn I could see two of the runners in front of me began to lose their strides. Their legs were cramping up. By contrast, I felt like a colt. I knew Fleetfoot must be running near my tail.

I surged into the home stretch. I could hear the pounding feet and exploding breaths close behind me. Then the crowd's roar erased any other sound.

The tape appeared in a shimmering blue -- so far ahead. Suddenly, hot pain seared my lungs. Muscles screamed in my legs. My body demanded a stop to this punishment. But, I kicked even harder. I hoped Fleetfoot was suffering as painfully too. "You must run through it," the coaches had often said. "You must drive through the pain." I knew they were right.

Trainers and teammates grabbed me just past the finish to keep me from falling. They held me up shouting. "You did it. You won."

"You won!"

Sheer happiness kept the gorge in my throat. I won. People joyously pounded my back. I won!

A judge with a stopwatch and clipboard stood in front of me and shouted officiously, "I've got this gentleman in first, number 514 of Northwestern -- congratulations son!"

I shook my head in amazement. Yes, I had finished first. I grabbed the official's arm and gasped. "I did it. I did it. I beat Frank Fleetfoot!"

His face quickly clouded over. He let his stopwatch dangle from his neck and patted my hand. "I'm afraid not son. You won but you didn't beat Fleetfoot. You see, his shorts fell off at the start of the race."

Like most major Universities, the greater proportion of our student athletes attended school on athletic scholarships that paid for tuition, sometimes room and board, books and a few incidentals. It depended a great deal on the particular sport and your expertise, but most of us got along without too much strain. One thing we members of the football team were sure of -- we earned those scholarships.

Oh sure, we liked football, however Northwestern confronted (I can't bring myself to write "played") the toughest teams in the country and if the confrontations weren't brutal enough, the daily three hour practices were symphonies of blood-letting. I mean there was some real hitting going on throughout the fall, and a good part of the spring.

Some mornings, my fraternity brothers had to help me out of bed. I couldn't move my bruised body until they got me upright. Yes, we invested a lot of work, sweat, and pain for those scholarships.

241

Most of the time, the University community seemed to appreciate our efforts. We were at least mildly admired, especially because our School's high academic standards kept any "cement-heads" from staying around more than a few months.

About once a year though, someone in the Administrative Office, or perhaps it was a Professor who had never raised a drop of perspiration, began to worry that we athletes were getting too much. We should do some formal work, above and beyond getting our noses broken, fingers snapped, or teeth bashed out.

It was in the spring when word first came from the "front office," that I was to report there when I had "spare time." I felt irritated. All I had for the spring quarter was football, track, and nineteen tough credits.

Well, I showed up when I could, and sorted registration cards. I made green piles, red piles, blue piles, yellow piles, and taller white piles. One of the secretaries even complimented me on my work. "You're quite bright for a football player." Being a gentleman, I quoted long passages from Shakespeare, verbatim, rather than feeding her the registration cards.

Apparently, some other gridiron warriors, incensed at this "Mickey Mouse" assignment, had purposely fouled up the building of colored piles, and been dismissed from doing any more "office work." I even got to do some filing during the month I was on the job.

A year later, the "word" came down from on high, again. Our group was ordered to report to the Buildings and Grounds Department. The guys in B and G didn't have much formal education, so they were pretty nice. They simply knew they had to put us to work, somewhere on the campus, and we were told orders stated we should be kept busy for a couple of months.

Our first job consisted of trimming the hedges around the Technological Institute. Now, the Tech Building was one of the most beautiful at Northwestern. I remember how its massive yet tasteful architecture had impressed me during my initial recruiting visit. Huge thick hedges extending

243

outward in the front, added a breathtaking depth of natural beauty. It was definitely a showplace.

The B and G supervisors gave about twenty-five of us hedge-clippers, and told us to square off the greenery. We were strong as stallions, but few of us had ever even held a large hedge-clipper before. Add to our inexperience the fact that some of us were forced to balance on stepladders to reach the ten-foot tops, and anyone could see we had big problems. It also was tough work, cutting through those branches.

We hadn't been given any instructions or guidance. In a little while we became discouraged. the protests of the athletes who were miffed at having been forced to do any of this, as they put it "idiot work," began to get more attention. I assumed they were among those who mixed up the multi-colored cards the year before. The more obvious it became that we lacked the skill to do a decent job, the closer we approached open revolt.

A defensive end cut a hole from the other side of one of the thicker hedges and yelled, "Peekaboo, I see you." I stared at him in disbelief while he widened the circumference of his tunnel, until he could crawl all the way through it.

One of our star halfbacks gleefully chopped the manicured corner off one of the tallest hedgerows, almost toppling from his ladder in the process. Secure on his perch again, he raised the big shears over his head with a yell. It came as sort of a signal, like a bugle call sounds the charge.

Most of us cheered, then began hacking away with a vengeance. Leaves, large twigs, even thick branches flew through the air. "Chop, chop, chop, chop," we chanted like maniacs. It took only a couple of hours to desecrate nature's decorative trim in front of this temple of learning.

None had been chopped down all the way. Oh no, that would have been too tidy. Instead, those once stately rows had been reduced to gruesome configurations. There were jagged cones, and yards of six-inch stubble, four ten-foot pillars, obvious phallic symbols, and a long green ski-slope profile which began with a huge cleft in the shape of a "V" for victory.

When one of the guys from B and G came by to check on us, he was so startled by the scene, he ran his jeep into a curb, tipped it on its side, and was thrown out. We helped him up and righted the vehicle.

Neither he nor the jeep seemed damaged in any way. In fact, he didn't seem concerned about his slight mishap at all. He just kept staring at our handiwork shaking his head in disbelief and muttering, "Madonna, y Santa Theresa -- Oh, Madonna, Madonna!"

Since he seemed a religious man, we left him to his prayers and quietly placed our hedge-cutters in the back of his jeep. An offensive tackle tried to console him with "Dominus Vobiscum, Amigo," but he failed to react, merely continuing to mutter "Madonna, Madonna." We headed up Sheridan Road to catch the green bus that would take us to football practice.

Did I say that was our first job
for "Buildings and Grounds?" It
turned out to be the last. In fact,
we were never asked to do "idiot
work," again.

"We want to be able to tell everyone, students, alumni, friends - that our entire football team made a financial contribution to the University during its Centennial Year," announced the guy from the Public Relations Office. he said it with conviction, but sweat was pouring down his face. After all he wore a double-breasted suit, and most of us were naked or sitting around in jocks. The locker room smelled awful.

"You should have waited until after we had our showers," someone yelled out. Everybody laughed.

The guy from the P.R. office smiled nervously. "I'll just leave this basket on the table here and you fellows each contribute what you can afford. "And thank you," he called out as he took off in a hasty retreat.

All the coaches quickly left the Purple Locker room. After some mild cussing, the room became eerily quiet. I supposed every guy was searching his soul.

My locker was next to Jasper K. Bigbucks, Jr., a third string end. He once told me his father was a surgeon. "Gee, that's really something," he mused, "Northwestern's one-hundred years old - began in 1851."

"Yes," I agreed, "that's mighty impressive."

"I don't know what to contribute," he said, reaching into his locker and bringing out his checkbook. "How much are you going to give?"

"Well, I really haven't decided," I lied. I knew I had $2.65 in my trousers. "I'll think it over in the shower."

He energetically wrote a check, peeled it out of his checkbook, and handed it to me. "Do you think this is all right?"

His check read, "Pay to the Order of Northwestern University = $1,000." I swallowed hard and said, "Sure, Jas, I think that should do it fine."

He smiled contentedly.

Later, I was the sixth one who dove into the backseat of a battered car, heading back to campus. I pulled in my legs and someone shut the door.

"Hey, Riordan, how much did you contribute to the Centennial Fund?"

"Well," I answered, "Jasper and I contributed an average of 501 dollars a piece."

"Someone shouted, "You bullcrapper."

Another one said, "We didn't know your folks had money. Besides, you don't even have a checking account."

"Check, hell," I replied, "with me it's strictly cash."

They all laughed, and a muscular arm shot out and opened the car door. "Rich kids walk," they yelled, and a jumble of strong hands and arms tried to push me out.

My feet dragged all the way back to campus, but with considerable effort I managed to keep my head and shoulders in the car.

"Let's have something really special for dessert," said Norris Fester, "I'm still hungry."

"Sounds great to me," I replied.

We were in a Chicago French restaurant, celebrating Fester's acceptance in the Army as a Lieutenant. He loosened his tie and half-rising in his seat yelled out, "Garkon, garkon! Where the hell is our waiter?"

I tried to tactfully point out this was a distinguished French restaurant, and waiters were really French. I also explained that the word for waiter was pronounced "garçon" with a soft "s sound," because the "c" in the middle of the word had a cedille under it.

"Oh yeah?" said Norris, "well you can stuff that crap. I'm paying for the dinner and it's costing a bundle. Garkon, garkon," he shouted, snapping his fingers, "toot sweet. Hey, how's that for spouting French?"

I tried to hide behind my napkin.

Our waiter arrived and bowed, obviously quite irritated, "Oui Monsieur?"

"We'd like some of that French pastry."

"Oui monsieur," replied the waiter and he quickly brought a half-filled pastry cart to our table.

"Naw, naw," said Fester, "I want that filled one over there. It's got a better selection.

With another bow, our waiter removed the half-filled pastry cart and wheeled over a magnificent five-tiered cart that had not been touched. He said, "Please enjoy, monsieurs." Then he left, apparently not wishing to serve us.

"Wow, this looks terrific!" I observed. There were five full tiers of luscious creations; many of chocolate, some of chocolate and fudge, chocolate and cherries, chocolate and strawberries, fudge and cream, eclairs, and carefully crafted tarts.

"Which one do you want Norris?"

"What do you mean 'which one?'"

"Well," I tried to explain, "you're supposed to take one. If the one you want is closer to me, I'll pass it to you."

Fester shook his head, "I told you I was still hungry." He began setting the delicacies on our table. "Help yourself," he said.

We slowly demolished all five tiers of French pastry. We ate everything. The cart was absolutely bare.

When our waiter returned eventually, -- "Ah monsieurs, will there...." -- his mouth dropped open in mid-sentence. He did a double take from our empty pastry cart, to both of us, and stared back at the cart. His lips quivered and a tick began jumping near his left eye. With great difficulty he cleared his throat, "Sacre bleu, cochons, cochons, cochons." The tick became more agitated, and with an obvious effort at self control, he almost ran for the kitchen. He didn't come out. Norris had to pay the Maitre d'.

After the parking attendant brought our car, and Fester was settled behind the wheel, he asked, "What the hell was all the fuss about back there?"

"Well," I began, "I guess it's customary to take only one piece of French pastry."

"Yeah? So what? I left him a buck tip."

I stared straight ahead through the windshield.

Fester swung onto Michigan Avenue. "What was that word he said before he ran for the kitchen?" he asked with a grin.

"I believe it was 'cochon.'" I coughed momentarily. "It means 'pig' in French."

"Oh yeah," said Fester, "those damn foreigners. They're going to ruin this country."

After Hank graduated, and became Jeffrey Hunter of the movies, probably the best looking Brother in our House was Bob. For over a year he was definitely the handsomest in a Fraternity that had a reputation for good looking members.

He'd been, and still was, a fighter pilot, now in the Navy Reserve. Bob looked like a fighter pilot, tall, slender, blond curly-haired, with long lashed sky-blue eyes that seemed to take in everything. I've known a number of fighter pilots who didn't look at all like fighter jockeys. But, if you'd put Bob in a room with thirty other guys you'd invariably pick him out as a bona fide fighter pilot.

Of course, the ladies loved him, however, while he dated, he always was an extremely serious student following a tough engineering major. "The day I graduate from Northwestern is going to be one of the proudest of my life," he said at least a couple of times.

With all his studies, he still found time to see a lot of Jane, one of the real campus beauties. They made a devastating looking couple.

He appeared to be extremely happy as our final quarter progressed, but about a month before graduation he became moody and apprehensive.

"Are <u>your</u> folks coming to the graduation ceremonies?" he asked.

"Oh sure, they're looking forward to it. My brother's coming, too. Your folks going to make it?"

"Well I think so," he answered pensively, anyway they want to come."

"It sounds as if there's some problem." I observed.

"Well there is," he admitted lighting a cigarette. "I'm engaged to two different women, one here and one from home."

"Oh, oh, and to think I used to want to have your problems."

"Yeh, well you wouldn't want to have this one. It's funny," he mused, "Jane and I never exchanged pins, and I never gave my hometown girl a ring, they just both assumed we were getting married."

"Maybe when they meet at graduation they'll like each other," I commented.

"Not funny, Lee. What am I going to do?"

I couldn't come up with an answer but I came to the conclusion that being super good looking often led to trouble.

Bob arranged a bogus California job interview for the day of graduation. His folks and both his girls were disappointed, however, I guess they all understood the importance of securing a good job.

Sometime after the graduation ceremonies, Bob called me at the House.

"How did it go?"

"Fine! I graduated and so did you. Say, are you really in California?"

"Sure I am," exhulted Bob, "just outside Los Angeles, and what's more I got the job!"

"What do you mean you got the job? There wasn't any."

"Well there is now, things really happen fast out here, I'm

starting next week. And, there's something else besides."

"What's that?"

"I'll write you. I've got to get going and buy an engagement ring!"

A GIFT TO POSTERITY

There were showers on every floor of our fraternity house, except the first. They were put to almost constant use. We certainly were a clean bunch of guys. Some showered twice a day, a few three times.

Many modern psychiatrists say taking a lot of showers means a "masturbation complex," but I doubt that was the case where we were concerned. Besides, not only, was sex almost nonexistent on campus, there wasn't really any place to masturbate. Oh I suppose if you wanted to badly enough, you could have gone downstairs in our house on a Sunday morning about 4:00 a.m. and been alone, but that would have meant very careful planning and a loss of sleep.

At home I never felt particularly dirty. I couldn't see taking more than one shower per day. During the year at school, my single shower often came after an athletic practice, football in fall, wrestling in winter, and track during the spring months.

Now and then, I did enjoy soothing my aching muscles in a hot tub-bath. A few more of the Brothers did, too. We didn't admit this openly, but kept our penchant for soaking strictly among ourselves. Showers were Macho. Tub-baths definitely were not. Rumor had it that the upper reaches of sorority houses were full of bathtubs, but our single one sat in an inconspicuous corner of the fourth floor lavatory. Only three Brothers lived up there, so it was pretty private.

A few times a week, I fervently enjoyed a "warm-tub," as the British say. My muscles and brain really relaxed while I reposed in the circulating hot water, perusing a book or magazine. I always took something to read. In fact, all of us did.

Naturally, we had a scheduling problem. Since there was only one unit, reservations were necessary. A user certainly wanted to count on at least a half hour of uninterrupted bliss. So, a timetable was arranged for a week in advance.

We also shared a common difficulty. None of us could come up with an efficient way to handle reading material while bathing. Lighter paperbacks and the Reader's Digest were no problem, however larger magazines and textbooks cramped one's arms after fifteen minutes or so. A few even fell into the water. We tried to figure out some solution.

There didn't seem to be any. Oh we rigged clotheslines, and erected various complicated wire devices, but nothing actually worked for any length of time. The books and magazines continued getting wet, and our arms grew tired from holding them up.

Suddenly, I thought of an answer to the predicament. No, it wasn't a quick solution, and it wasn't for us, but for future Brothers, for posterity. We changed part of our rules. Instead of cleaning out the entire tub after we were through, we left the dirty ring that formed inside the upper edge.

I reasoned, and my cohorts agreed unanimously, if we never touched the ring, eventually it would thicken. Every time we took a bath, each one of us would contribute and some day a ridge would form, wide enough for a bather to rest his elbows on. He could read his volume in absolute comfort while enjoying the hot water. It should be perfect bliss.

True, since we only had four or fewer years to work on the project it never could be for us. Nevertheless, maybe not the next class, nor the next, nor the next, but some future bunch of guys would benefit from our efforts.

We erected a framed testimonial, explaining our endeavor along with the date and our signatures. It hung right over the tub. We hoped this would create a kind of immortality for us in our Fraternity, and among those fortunate Brothers, whose bathing was yet to come.

Each one of the current bathers strictly kept the pact. We never disturbed the ring. Almost imperceptively, it continued to accumulate.

On a hot June day, my graduation day from Northwestern University, I climbed up to the fourth floor still in my robes to examine our tub. I carried a small plastic ruler with me so I could measure carefully and accurately. What I found, made me proud. The ring had grown to nearly a quarter of an inch.

Additional copies are available at selected book stores and by

-- MAIL --

$8.95 each (includes postage and handling) <u>from</u> the author (check or money order, please)

Lee Riordan
P.O. Box 93111
Milwaukee, WI 53203

Name.............................

Address..........................

City.............................

State................Zip.........

# of copies......................

Amount enclosed $................